Research Methodology

Published by
Saurabh Publishing House

Research Methodolgy

Dr. Debashis Chakraborty

Saurabh
Publishing House
4735/22, Prakash Deep Building,
Ansari Road, Daryaganj
New Delhi- 110002

Published by
SAURABH PUBLISHING HOUSE

Distributed by:
Lotus Press Publishers & Distributors
Unit No. 220, Second Floor, 4735/22, Prakash Deep Building,
Ansari Road, Darya Ganj, New Delhi-110002
Ph: 23280047, 32903912, 098118-38000
www.lotuspress.co.in

Saurabh Publishing is an imprint of
Lotus Press Publishers & Distributors

Research Methodology

ISBN 978-81-89005-27-6

Printed at: **Afcons Enterprises, New Delhi**

Preface

Research is the cornerstone of any science, including both the hard sciences such as chemistry or physics and the soft sciences such as psychology, management or education. It refers to the organised, structured, and purposeful attempt aimed at discovering, interpreting, and revising human knowledge on different aspects of the world.

The goal of the research process is to produce new knowledge, which takes three main forms: exploratory research, which structures and identifies new problems; constructive research, which develops solutions to a problem and empirical research, which tests the feasibility of a solution using empirical evidence. Research methods used by scholars include action research, cartography, case study, classification, experiments, interviews, mathematical models, participant observation, simulation, statistical analysis, statistical surveys and so on.

This book is designed specifically for students with no previous experience or knowledge of research methods. It is a comprehensive work written in a lucid style, in simple language and with examples. It is hoped that this book will be of immense use and fill in the gapes between theory and practice to research scholars of various disciplines.

Author

Contents

1

Introduction

Research is a human activity based on intellectual investigation and is aimed at discovering, interpreting, and revising human knowledge on different aspects of the world. Research can use the scientific method, but need not do so. Scientific research relies on the application of the scientific method, a harnessing of curiosity. This research provides scientific information and theories for the explanation of the nature and the properties of the world around us. It makes practical applications possible. Scientific research is funded by public authorities, by charitable organisations and by private groups, including many companies. Scientific research can be subdivided into different classifications.

FUNDAMENTAL RESEARCH

Basic research has as its primary objective the advancement of knowledge and the theoretical understanding of the relations among variables. It is exploratory and often driven by the researcher's curiosity, interest, and intuition. It is conducted without any practical end in mind, although it may have unexpected results pointing to practical applications. The terms "basic" or "fundamental" indicate that, through theory generation, basic research provides the foundation for further, sometimes applied research. As there is no guarantee of short-term practical gain, researchers may find it difficult to obtain funding for basic research. Research is a subset of invention.

Traditionally, basic research was considered as an activity that preceded applied research, which in turn preceded development into practical applications. Recently, these distinctions have become much less clear-cut, and it is sometimes the case that all stages will intermix. This is particularly the case in fields such as biotechnology and electronics, where fundamental discoveries may be made alongside work intended to develop new products, and in areas where public and private sector partners collaborate in order to develop greater insight into key areas of interest. For this reason, some now prefer the term frontier research.

RESEARCH PROCESSES

Scientific Research

Generally, research is understood to follow a certain structural process. Though step order may vary depending on the subject matter and researcher, the following steps are usually part of most formal research, both basic and applied:

- — Formation of the topic.
- — Hypothesis.
- — Conceptual definitions.
- — Operational definitions.
- — Gathering of data.
- — Analysis of data.

— Test, revising of hypothesis.

— Conclusion, iteration if necessary.

A common misunderstanding is that by this method a hypothesis can be proven. Generally a hypothesis is used to make predictions that can be tested by observing the outcome of an experiment. If the outcome is inconsistent with the hypothesis, then the hypothesis is rejected. However, if the outcome is consistent with the hypothesis, the experiment is said to support the hypothesis. This careful language is used because researchers recognise that alternative hypotheses may also be consistent with the observations.

In this sense, a hypothesis can never be proven, but rather only supported by surviving rounds of scientific testing and, eventually, becoming widely thought of as true, but this is not the same as it having been proven. A useful hypothesis allows prediction and within the accuracy of observation of the time, the prediction will be verified. As the accuracy of observation improves with time, the hypothesis may no longer provide an accurate prediction. In this case a new hypothesis will arise to challenge the old, and to the extent that the new hypothesis makes more accurate predictions than the old, the new will supplant it.

Historical Method

The historical method comprises the techniques and guidelines by which historians use historical sources and other evidence to research and then to write history. There are various history guidelines commonly used by historians in their work, under the headings of external criticism, internal criticism, and synthesis. This includes higher criticism and textual criticism. Though items may vary depending on the subject matter and researcher, the following concepts are usually part of most formal historical research:

— Identification of origin date.

— Evidence of localisation.

— Recognition of authorship.

— Analysis of data.

— Identification of integrity.

— Attribution of credibility.

RESEARCH METHODS

The goal of the research process is to produce new knowledge, which takes three main forms:

— Exploratory research, which structures and identifies new problems.

— Constructive research, which develops solutions to a problem.

— Empirical research, which tests the feasibility of a solution using empirical evidence.

Research can also fall into two distinct types:

— Primary research.

— Secondary research.

Research methods used by scholars include:

— Action research.

— Cartography.

— Case study.

— Classification.

— Experience and intuition.

— Experiments.

— Interviews.

— Mathematical models.

— Participant observation.

— Simulation.
— Statistical analysis.
— Statistical surveys.
— Content or Textual Analysis.
— Ethnography.

Research is often conducted using the hourglass model. The hourglass model starts with a broad spectrum for research, focusing in on the required information through the methodology of the project, then expands the research in the form of discussion and results.

ACADEMIC PUBLISHING

Academic publishing describes a system that is necessary in order for academic scholars to peer review the work and make it available for a wider audience. The 'system', which is probably disorganised enough not to merit the title, varies widely by field, and is also always changing, if often slowly. Most academic work is published in journal article or book form.

In publishing, STM publishing is an abbreviation for academic publications in science, technology, and medicine. Most established academic fields have their own journals and other outlets for publication, though many academic journals are somewhat interdisciplinary, and publish work from several distinct fields or subfields. The kinds of publications that are accepted as contributions of knowledge or research vary greatly between fields.

Academic publishing is undergoing major changes, emerging from the transition from the print to the electronic format. Business models are different in the electronic environment. Since about the early 1990s, licensing of electronic resources, particularly journals, has been very common. Presently, a major trend, particularly with respect to scholarly journals, is open access. There are two main forms of open access: open access publishing, in which the articles or the whole journal is freely available from the time of publication, and self-archiving, where the author makes a copy of their own work freely available on the web.

FUNDING FOR SCIENTIFIC RESEARCH

Most funding for scientific research comes from two major sources, corporations and government. Many senior researchers spend more than a trivial amount of their time applying for grants for research funds. These grants are necessary not only for researchers to carry out their research, but also as a source of merit. Some faculty positions require that the holder has received grants from certain institutions.

ISSUES IN RESEARCH

This section provides an overview the major issues in research and in evaluation. This is probably the best place for you to begin learning about research. We have to begin somewhere. (Although, if you think about it, the whole idea of hyperlinked text sort of runs contrary to the notion that there is a single place to begin — you can begin anywhere, go anywhere, and leave anytime. Unfortunately, you can only be in one place at a time and, even less fortunately for you, you happen to be right here right now, so we may as well consider this a place to begin.) And what better place to begin than an introduction? Here's where we take care of all the stuff you think you already know, and probably should already know, but most likely don't know as well as you think you do.

The first thing we have to get straight is the language of research. If we don't, we're going to have a hard time discussing research. With the basic terminology under our belts, we can look a little more deeply at some of the underlying philosophical issues that drive the research endeavour. We also need to recognise that social research always occurs in a social context. It is a human endeavour. Therefore, it's important to consider the critical ethical issues that affect the researcher, research participants, and the research effort generally.

LANGUAGE OF RESEARCH

Learning about research is a lot like learning about anything else. To start, you need to learn the jargon people use, the big controversies they fight over, and the different factions that define the major players. We'll start by considering five really big multi-syllable words that researchers sometimes use to describe what they do. We'll only do a few for now, to give you an idea of just how esoteric the discussion can get. We can then take on some of the major issues in research like the types of questions we can ask in a project, the role of time in research, and the different types of relationships we can estimate.

Then we have to consider defining some basic terms like variable, hypothesis, data, and unit of analysis. If you're like me, you hate learning vocabulary, so we'll quickly move along to consideration of two of the major fallacies of research, just to give you an idea of how wrong even researchers can be if they're not careful. Research involves an eclectic blending of an enormous range of skills and activities. To be a good social researcher, you have to be able to work well with a wide variety of people, understand the specific methods used to conduct research, understand the subject that you are studying, be able to convince someone to give you the funds to study it, stay on track and on schedule, speak and write persuasively, and on and on.

Types of Questions

There are three basic types of questions that research projects can address:

1. *Descriptive*: When a study is designed primarily to describe what is going on or what exists. Public opinion polls that seek only to describe the proportion of people who hold various opinions are primarily descriptive in nature. For instance, if we want to know what percent of the population would vote for U.P.A or N.D.A. in the next general election, we are simply interested in describing something.
2. *Relational*: When a study is designed to look at the relationships between two or more variables. A public opinion poll that compares what proportion of males and females say they would vote for a Congress or a B.J.P. candidate in the next general election in India is essentially studying the relationship between gender and voting preference.
3. *Causal*: When a study is designed to determine whether one or more variables causes or affects one or more outcome variables. If we did a public opinion poll to try to determine whether a recent political advertising campaign changed voter preferences, we would essentially be studying whether the campaign changed the proportion of voters who would vote U.P.A. or N.D.A.

The three question types can be viewed as cumulative. That is, a relational study assumes that you can first describe each of the variables you are trying to relate. And, a causal study assumes that you can describe both the cause and effect variables and that you can show that they are related to each other. Causal studies are probably the most demanding of the three.

TIME IN RESEARCH DESIGN

Time is an important element of any research design, and here we want to introduce one of the most fundamental distinctions in research design nomenclature: cross-sectional versus longitudinal studies. A cross-sectional study is one that takes place at a single point in time. In effect, we are taking a 'slice' or cross-section of whatever it is we're observing or measuring.

A longitudinal study is one that takes place over time — we have at least two waves of measurement in a longitudinal design. A further distinction is made between two types of longitudinal designs: repeated measures and time series. There is no universally agreed upon rule for distinguishing these two terms, but in general, if you have two or a few waves of measurement, you are using a repeated measures design.

If you have many waves of measurement over time, you have a time series. Usually, we wouldn't use the term time series unless we had at least twenty waves of measurement, and often far more. Sometimes the way we distinguish these is with the analysis methods we would use. Time series analysis requires that you have at least twenty or so observations. Repeated measures analyses aren't often used with as many as twenty waves of measurement.

TYPES OF RELATIONSHIPS

A relationship refers to the correspondence between two variables. When we talk about types of relationships, we can mean that in at least two ways: the nature of the relationship or the pattern of it.

Nature of a Relationship

While all relationships tell about the correspondence

between two variables, there is a special type of relationship that holds that the two variables are not only in correspondence, but that one causes the other. This is the key distinction between a simple correlational relationship and a causal relationship. A correlational relationship simply says that two things perform in a synchronized manner. For instance, we often talk of a correlation between inflation and unemployment. When inflation is high, unemployment also tends to be high. When inflation is low, unemployment also tends to be low.

The two variables are correlated. But knowing that two variables are correlated does not tell us whether one *causes* the other. We know, for instance, that there is a correlation between the number of roads built in Europe and the number of children born in the United States. Does that mean that is we want fewer children in the U.S., we should stop building so many roads in Europe? Or, does it mean that if we don't have enough roads in Europe, we should encourage U.S. citizens to have more babies? Of course not.

While there is a relationship between the number of roads built and the number of babies, we don't believe that the relationship is a causal one. This leads to consideration of what is often termed the third variable problem. In this example, it may be that there is a third variable that is causing both the building of roads and the birthrate, that is causing the correlation we observe. For instance, perhaps the general world economy is responsible for both. When the economy is good more roads are built in Europe and more children are born in the U.S. The key lesson here is that you have to be careful when you interpret correlations.

If you observe a correlation between the number of hours students use the computer to study and their grade point averages, you cannot assume that the relationship is causal: that computer use improves grades. In this case, the third variable might be socioeconomic status — richer students who have greater resources at their disposal tend to both use computers and do better in their grades. It's the resources that drives both use and grades, not computer use that causes the change in the grade point average.

Relationship Patterns

We have several terms to describe the major different types of patterns one might find in a relationship. First, there is the case of no relationship at all. If you know the values on one variable, you don't know anything about the values on the other. For instance, we suspect that there is no relationship between the length of the lifeline on your hand and your grade point average. In a positive relationship, high values on one variable are associated with high values on the other and low values on one are associated with low values on the other. In this example, we assume an idealised positive relationship between years of education and the salary one might expect to be making.

On the other hand a negative relationship implies that high values on one variable are associated with low values on the other. This is also sometimes termed an inverse relationship. Here, we show an idealised negative relationship between a measure of self esteem and a measure of paranoia in psychiatric patients. These are the simplest types of relationships we might typically estimate in research. But the pattern of a relationship can be more complex than this.

VARIABLES

You won't be able to do very much in research unless

you know how to talk about variables. A variable is any entity that can take on different values. OK, so what does that mean? Anything that can vary can be considered a variable. For instance, age can be considered a variable because age can take different values for different people or for the same person at different times. Similarly, country can be considered a variable because a person's country can be assigned a value.

Variables aren't always 'quantitative' or numerical. The variable 'gender' consists of two text values: 'male' and 'female'. We can, if it is useful, assign quantitative values instead of the text values, but we don't have to assign numbers in order for something to be a variable. It's also important to realise that variables aren't only things that we measure in the traditional sense. For instance, in much social research and in programme evaluation, we consider the treatment or programme to be made up of one or more variables. An educational programme can have varying amounts of 'time on task', 'classroom settings', 'student-teacher ratios', and so on. So even the programme can be considered a variable.

An attribute is a specific value on a variable. For instance, the variable sex or gender has two attributes: male and female. Or, the variable agreement might be defined as having five attributes:

— 1 = strongly disagree.

— 2 = disagree.

— 3 = neutral.

— 4 = agree.

— 5 = strongly agree.

Another important distinction having to do with the term 'variable' is the distinction between an independent and dependent variable. This distinction is particularly relevant when you are investigating cause-effect relationships. An independent variable was one that would be free to vary or respond to some programme or treatment, and that a dependent variable must be one that depends on the efforts. But this is entirely backwards! In fact the independent variable is what you (or nature) manipulates — a treatment or programme or cause.

The dependent variable is what is affected by the independent variable — your effects or outcomes. For example, if you are studying the effects of a new educational programme on student achievement, the programme is the independent variable and your measures of achievement are the dependent ones.

Finally, there are two traits of variables that should always be achieved. Each variable should be exhaustive, it should include all possible answerable responses. For instance, if the variable is "religion" and the only options are "Hindu", "Christian", and "Muslim", there are quite a few religions we can think of that haven't been included. The list does not exhaust all possibilities. On the other hand, if you exhaust all the possibilities with some variables — religion being one of them — you would simply have too many responses. The way to deal with this is to explicitly list the most common attributes and then use a general category like "Other" to account for all remaining ones.

In addition to being exhaustive, the attributes of a variable should be mutually exclusive, no respondent should be able to have two attributes simultaneously. While this might seem obvious, it is often rather tricky in practice. For instance, you might be tempted to represent the variable "Employment Status" with the two attributes "employed" and "unemployed." But these attributes are not necessarily mutually exclusive — a person who is looking for a second job while employed would be able to check both attributes! But don't we often use questions on surveys that ask the respondent to "check all that apply" and then list a series of categories? Yes, we do, but technically speaking, each of the categories in a question like that is its own variable and is treated dichotomously as either "checked" or "unchecked", attributes that are mutually exclusive.

HYPOTHESES

An hypothesis is a specific statement of prediction. It describes in concrete terms what you expect will happen in your study. Not all studies have hypotheses. Sometimes a study is designed to be exploratory. There is no formal hypothesis, and perhaps the purpose of the study is to explore some area more thoroughly in order to develop some specific hypothesis or prediction that can be tested in future research. A single study may have one or many hypotheses.

Actually, whenever we talk about an hypothesis, we are really thinking simultaneously about *two* hypotheses. Let's say that you predict that there will be a relationship between two variables in your study. The way we would formally set up the hypothesis test is to formulate two hypothesis statements, one that describes your prediction and one that describes all the other possible outcomes with respect to the hypothesized relationship. Your prediction is that variable A and variable B will be related.

Then the only other possible outcome would be that variable A and variable B are not related. Usually, we call the hypothesis that you support the alternative hypothesis, and we call the hypothesis that describes the remaining possible outcomes the null hypothesis. Sometimes we use a notation like H_A or H1 to represent the alternative hypothesis or your prediction, and H_O or H_O to represent the null case. You have to be careful here, though. In some studies, your prediction might very well be that there will be no difference or change.

In this case, you are essentially trying to find support for the null hypothesis and you are opposed to the alternative. If your prediction specifies a direction, and the null therefore is the no difference prediction and the prediction of the opposite direction, we call this a one-tailed hypothesis. For instance, let's imagine that you are investigating the effects of a new employee training programme and that you believe one of the outcomes will be that there will be less employee absenteeism. Your two hypotheses might be stated something like this:

The null hypothesis for this study is:

> H_O: As a result of the XYZ company employee training programme, there will either be no significant difference in employee absenteeism or there will be a significant *increase*.

which is tested against the alternative hypothesis:

> H_A: As a result of the XYZ company employee training programme, there will be a significant *decrease* in employee absenteeism.

In the figure below, we see this situation illustrated graphically. The alternative hypothesis — your prediction that the programme will decrease absenteeism — is shown there.

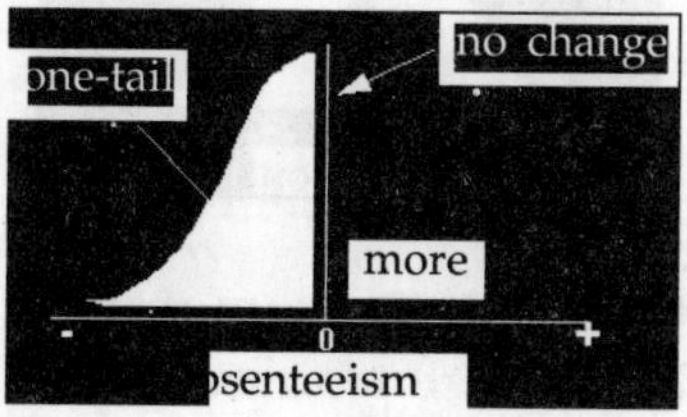

The null must account for the other two possible conditions: no difference, or an increase in absenteeism.

The figure shows a hypothetical distribution of absenteeism differences. We can see that the term "one-tailed" refers to the tail of the distribution on the outcome variable.

When your prediction does not specify a direction, we say you have a two-tailed hypothesis. For instance, let's assume you are studying a new drug treatment for depression. The drug has gone through some initial animal trials, but has not yet been tested on humans. You believe that the drug will have an effect, but you are not confident enough to hypothesise a direction and say the drug will reduce depression. In this case, you might state the two hypotheses like this:

The null hypothesis for this study is:

H_O: As a result of 300 mg./day of the ABC drug, there will be no significant difference in depression.

which is tested against the alternative hypothesis:

H_A: As a result of 300 mg./day of the ABC drug, there will be a significant difference in depression.

The figure below illustrates this two-tailed prediction for this case. Again, notice that the term "two-tailed" refers to the tails of the distribution for your outcome variable.

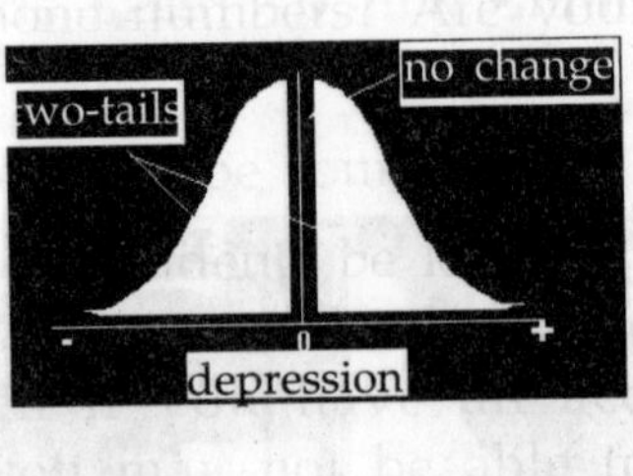

The important thing to remember about stating hypotheses is that you formulate your prediction, and then you formulate a second hypothesis that is mutually exclusive of the first and incorporates all possible alternative outcomes for that case. When your study analysis is completed, the idea is that you will have to choose between the two hypotheses. If your prediction was correct, then you would reject the null hypothesis and accept the alternative. If your original prediction was not supported in the data, then you will accept the null hypothesis and reject the alternative. The logic of hypothesis testing is based on these two basic principles:

— The formulation of two mutually exclusive hypothesis statements that, together, exhaust all possible outcomes.

— The testing of these so that one is necessarily accepted and the other rejected.

TYPES OF DATA

In some areas of social research, the qualitative-quantitative distinction has led to protracted arguments with the proponents of each arguing the superiority of their kind of data over the other. The quantitative types argue that their data is 'hard', 'rigorous', 'credible', and 'scientific'. The qualitative proponents counter that their data is 'sensitive', 'nuanced', 'detailed', and 'contextual'.

For many of us in social research, this kind of polarised debate has become less than productive. And, it obscures the fact that qualitative and quantitative data are intimately related to each other. All quantitative data is based upon qualitative judgements; and all qualitative data can be described and manipulated numerically. For instance, think about a very common quantitative measure in social research — a self-esteem scale.

The researchers who develop such instruments had to make countless judgments in constructing them: how to define self-esteem; how to distinguish it from other related concepts; how to word potential scale items; how to make sure the items would be understandable to the intended respondents; what kinds of contexts it could be used in; what kinds of cultural and language constraints might be present; and on and on. The researcher who decides to use such a scale in their study has to make another set of judgements: how well does the scale measure the intended concept; how reliable or consistent is it; how appropriate is it for the research context and intended respondents; and on and on.

Believe it or not, even the respondents make many judgments when filling out such a scale: what is meant by various terms and phrases; why is the researcher giving this scale to them; how much energy and effort do they want to expend to complete it, and so on. Even the consumers and readers of the research will make lots of judgements about the self-esteem measure and its appropriateness in that research context. What may look like a simple, straightforward, cut-and-dried quantitative measure is actually based on lots of qualitative judgments made by lots of different people.

On the other hand, all qualitative information can be easily converted into quantitative, and there are many times when doing so would add considerable value to your research. The simplest way to do this is to divide the qualitative information into units and number them! When we do something even as easy as this simple grouping or piling task, we can describe the results quantitatively.

UNIT OF ANALYSIS

One of the most important ideas in a research project is the unit of analysis. The unit of analysis is the major entity that you are analysing in your study. For instance, any of the following could be a unit of analysis in a study:

— Individuals.

— Groups.

— Artifacts (books, photos, newspapers).
— Geographical units (town, census tract, state).
— Social interactions (dyadic relations, divorces, arrests).

Why is it called the 'unit of analysis' and not something else (like, the unit of sampling)? Because it is the analysis you do in your study that determines what the unit is. For instance, if you are comparing the children in two classrooms on achievement test scores, the unit is the individual child because you have a score for each child. On the other hand, if you are comparing the two classes on classroom climate, your unit of analysis is the group, in this case the classroom, because you only have a classroom climate score for the class as a whole and not for each individual student.

For different analyses in the same study you may have different units of analysis. If you decide to base an analysis on student scores, the individual is the unit. But you might decide to compare average classroom performance. In this case, since the data that goes into the analysis is the average itself the unit of analysis is actually the group.

Even though you had data at the student level, you use aggregates in the analysis. In many areas of social research these hierarchies of analysis units have become particularly important and have spawned a whole area of statistical analysis sometimes referred to as hierarchical modelling. This is true in education, for instance, where we often compare classroom performance but collected achievement data at the individual student level.

RESEARCH FALLACIES

A fallacy is an error in reasoning, usually based on mistaken assumptions. Researchers are very familiar with all the ways they could go wrong, with the fallacies they are susceptible to. The ecological fallacy occurs when you make conclusions about individuals based only on analyses of group data. For instance, assume that you measured the math scores of a particular classroom and found that they had the highest average score in the district. Later you run into one of the kids from that class and you think to yourself "she must be a math whiz." Aha! Fallacy! Just because she comes from the class with the highest average doesn't mean that she is automatically a high-scorer in math. She could be the lowest math scorer in a class that otherwise consists of math geniuses!

An exception fallacy is sort of the reverse of the ecological fallacy. It occurs when you reach a group conclusion on the basis of exceptional cases. This is the kind of fallacious reasoning that is at the core of a lot of sexism and racism. The stereotype is of the guy who sees a woman make a driving error and concludes that "women are terrible drivers." Wrong! Fallacy! Both of these fallacies point to some of the traps that exist in both research and everyday reasoning.

2

Philosophy of Research

A research project has a well-known structure—a beginning, middle and end. We introduce the basic phases of a research project in The Structure of Research. In that section, we also introduce some important distinctions in research: the different types of questions you can ask in a research project; and, the major components or parts of a research project. Before the modern idea of research emerged, we had a term for what philosophers used to call research—logical reasoning. So, it should come as no surprise that some of the basic distinctions in logic have carried over into contemporary research.

In Systems of Logic we discuss how two major logical systems, the inductive and deductive methods of reasoning, are related to modern research. No introduction would be complete without considering something having to do with assumptions and philosophy. All research is based on assumptions about how the world is perceived and how we can best come to understand it. Of course, nobody really knows how we can best understand the world, and philosophers have been arguing about that very question for at least two millennia now, so all we're going to do is look at how most contemporary social scientists approach the question of how we know about the world around us. We consider two major philosophical schools of thought—Positivism and Post-Positivism—that are especially important perspectives for contemporary social research.

RESEARCH STRUCTURE

Most research projects share the same general structure. You might think of this structure as following the shape of an hourglass. The research process usually starts with a broad area of interest, the initial problem that the researcher wishes to study. For instance, the researcher could be interested in how to use computers to improve the performance of students in mathematics. But this initial interest is far too broad to study in any single research project.

The researcher has to narrow the question down to one that can reasonably be studied in a research project. This might involve formulating a hypothesis or a focus question. For instance, the researcher might hypothesize that a particular method of computer instruction in math will improve the ability of elementary school students in a specific district. At the narrowest point of the research hourglass, the researcher is engaged in direct measurement or observation of the question of interest.

Once the basic data is collected, the researcher begins to try to understand it, usually by analysing it in a variety of ways. Even for a single hypothesis there are a number of analyses a researcher might typically conduct. At this point, the researcher begins to formulate some initial conclusions about what happened as a result of the computerised math programme. Finally, the researcher often will attempt to address the original broad question of interest by generalising from the results of this specific study to other related situations. For instance, on the basis of strong results indicating that the math programme had a positive effect on student performance, the researcher might conclude that other school districts similar to the one in the study might expect similar results.

Basic Components of a Study

Here, we'll describe the basic components involved in a causal study. Because causal studies presuppose descriptive and relational questions, many of the components of causal studies will also be found in those others. Most social research originates from some general problem or question. You might, for instance, be interested in what programmes enable the unemployed to get jobs. Usually, the problem is broad enough that you could not hope to address it adequately in a single research study. Consequently, we typically narrow the problem down to a more specific research question that we can hope to address.

The research question is often stated in the context of some theory that has been advanced to address the problem. For instance, we might have the theory that ongoing support services are needed to assure that the newly employed remain employed. The research question is the central issue being addressed in the study and is often phrased in the language of theory. For instance, a research question might be:

> Is a programme of supported employment more effective (than no programme at all) at keeping newly employed persons on the job?

The problem with such a question is that it is still too general to be studied directly. Consequently, in most research we develop an even more specific statement, called an hypothesis that describes in operational terms exactly what we think will happen in the study. For instance, the hypothesis for our employment study might be something like:

> The Metropolitan Supported Employment Programme will significantly increase rates of employment after six months for persons who are newly employed (after being out of work for at least one year) compared with persons who receive no comparable programme.

Notice that this hypothesis is specific enough that a reader can understand quite well what the study is trying to assess. In causal studies, we have at least two major variables of interest, the cause and the effect. Usually the cause is some type of event, programme, or treatment. We make a distinction between causes that the researcher can control (such as a programme) versus causes that occur naturally or outside the researcher's influence (such as a change in interest rates, or the occurrence of an earthquake). The effect is the outcome that you wish to study.

For both the cause and effect we make a distinction between our idea of them (the construct) and how they are actually manifested in reality. For instance, when we think about what a programme of support services for the newly employed might be, we are thinking of the "construct." On the other hand, the real world is not always what we think it is. In research, we remind ourselves of this by distinguishing our view of an entity (the construct) from the entity as it exists (the operationalisation). Ideally, we would like the two to agree.

Social research is always conducted in a social context. We ask people questions, or observe families interacting, or measure the opinions of people in a city. An important component of a research project is the units that participate in the project. Units are directly related to the question of sampling. In most projects we cannot involve all of the people we might like to involve. For instance, in studying a programme of support services for the newly employed we can't possibly include in our study everyone in the world, or even in the country, who is newly employed. Instead, we have to try to obtain a representative sample of such people.

When sampling, we make a distinction between the theoretical population of interest to our study and the final sample that we actually measure in our study. Usually the term "units" refers to the people that we sample and from whom we gather information. But for some projects the units are organisations, groups, or geographical entities like cities or towns. Sometimes our sampling strategy is multi-level: we sample a number of cities and within them sample families. In causal studies, we are interested in the effects of some cause on one or more outcomes. The outcomes are directly related to the research problem—we are usually most interested in outcomes that are most reflective of the problem.

In our hypothetical supported employment study, we would probably be most interested in measures of employment—is the person currently employed, or, what is their rate of absenteeism. Finally, in a causal study we usually are comparing the effects of our cause of interest relative to other conditions. Thus, a key component in a causal study concerns how we decide what units receive our programme and which are placed in an alternative condition. This issue is directly related to the research design that we use in the study. One of the central questions in research design is determining how people wind up in or are placed in various programmes or treatments that we are comparing.

These, then, are the major components in a causal study:

— The Research Problem.

— The Research Question.

— The Programme (Cause).
— The Units.
— The Outcomes (Effect).
— The Design.

DEDUCTIVE AND INDUCTIVE APPROACHES

In logic, we often refer to the two broad methods of reasoning as the deductive and inductive approaches. Deductive reasoning works from the more general to the more specific. Sometimes this is informally called a "top-down" approach. We might begin with thinking up a theory about our topic of interest. We then narrow that down into more specific hypotheses that we can test. We narrow down even further when we collect observations to address the hypotheses. This ultimately leads us to be able to test the hypotheses with specific data—a confirmation of our original theories.

Inductive reasoning works the other way, moving from specific observations to broader generalisations and theories. Informally, we sometimes call this a "bottom up" approach. In inductive reasoning, we begin with specific observations and measures, begin to detect patterns and regularities, formulate some tentative hypotheses that we can explore, and finally end up developing some general conclusions or theories. These two methods of reasoning have a very different "feel" to them when you're conducting research. Inductive reasoning, by its very nature, is more open-ended and exploratory, especially at the beginning.

Deductive reasoning is more narrow in nature and is concerned with testing or confirming hypotheses. Even though a particular study may look like it's purely deductive, most social research involves both inductive and deductive reasoning processes at some time in the project. In fact, it doesn't take a rocket scientist to see that we could assemble the two graphs above into a single circular one that continually cycles from theories down to observations and back up again to theories. Even in the most constrained experiment, the researchers may observe patterns in the data that lead them to develop new theories.

POSITIVISM AND POST-POSITIVISM

Let's start our very brief discussion of philosophy of science with a simple distinction between epistemology and methodology. The term epistemology comes from the Greek word epistêmê, their term for knowledge. In simple terms, epistemology is the philosophy of knowledge or of how we come to know. Methodology is also concerned with how we come to know, but is much more practical in nature. Methodology is focused on the specific ways—the methods—that we can use to try to understand our world better.

Epistemology and methodology are intimately related: the former involves the philosophy of how we come to know the world and the latter involves the practice. When most people in our society think about science, they think about some guy in a white lab coat working at a lab bench mixing up chemicals. They think of science as boring, cut-and-dry, and they think of the scientist as narrow-minded and esoteric. A lot of our stereotypes about science come from a period where science was dominated by a particular philosophy—positivism—that tended to support some of these views.

Let's begin by considering what positivism is. In its broadest sense, positivism is a rejection of metaphysics. It is a position that holds that the goal of knowledge is simply to describe the phenomena that we experience. The purpose of science is simply to stick to what we can observe and measure. Knowledge of anything beyond that, a positivist would hold, is impossible. When we think of positivism, we think of the behaviourists in mid-20th century psychology. These were the mythical 'rat runners' who believed that psychology could only study what could be directly observed and measured. Since we can't directly observe emotions, thoughts, etc., these were not legitimate topics for a scientific psychology.

In a positivist view of the world, science was seen as the way to get at truth, to understand the world well enough so that we might predict and control it. The world and the universe were deterministic—they operated by laws of cause and effect that we could discern if we applied the unique approach of the scientific method. Science was largely a mechanistic or mechanical affair. We use deductive reasoning to postulate theories that we can test. Based on the results of our studies, we may learn that our theory doesn't fit the facts well and so we need to revise our theory to better predict reality.

The positivist believed in empiricism—the idea that observation and measurement was the core of the scientific endeavour. The key approach of the scientific method is the experiment, the attempt to discern natural laws through direct manipulation and observation. Things have changed in our views of science since the middle part of the 20th century. Probably the most important has been our shift away from positivism into what we term post-positivism.

A post-positivist might begin by recognising that the way scientists think and work and the way we think in our everyday life are not distinctly different. Scientific reasoning and common sense reasoning are essentially the same process. There is no difference in kind between the two, only a difference in degree.

One of the most common forms of post-positivism is a philosophy called critical realism. A critical realist believes that there is a reality independent of our thinking about it that science can study. Positivists were also realists. The difference is that the post-positivist critical realist recognises that all observation is fallible and has error and that all theory is revisable. In other words, the critical realist is critical of our ability to know reality with certainty.

Where the positivist believed that the goal of science was to uncover the truth, the post-positivist critical realist believes that the goal of science is to hold steadfastly to the goal of getting it right about reality, even though we can never achieve that goal! Because all measurement is fallible, the post-positivist emphasises the importance of multiple measures and observations, each of which may possess different types of error, and the need to use triangulation across these multiple errorful sources to try to get a better bead on what's happening in reality.

The post-positivist also believes that all observations are theory-laden and that scientists are inherently biased by their cultural experiences, world views, and so on. Post-positivism rejects the relativist idea of the incommensurability of different perspectives, the idea that we can never understand each other because we come from different experiences and cultures. Most post-positivists are constructivists who believe that we each construct our view of the world based on our perceptions of it. Because perception and observation is fallible, our constructions must be imperfect.

Positivists believed that objectivity was a characteristic that resided in the individual scientist. Scientists are responsible for putting aside their biases and beliefs and seeing the world as it 'really' is. Post-positivists reject the idea that any individual can see the world perfectly as it really is. We are all biased and all of our observations are affected. Our best hope for achieving objectivity is to triangulate across multiple fallible perspectives! Thus, objectivity is not the characteristic of an individual, it is inherently a social phenomenon. It is what multiple individuals are trying to achieve when they criticize each other's work.

We never achieve objectivity perfectly, but we can approach it. The best way for us to improve the objectivity of what we do is to do it within the context of a broader contentious community of truth-seekers who criticize each other's work. The theories that survive such intense scrutiny are a bit like the species that survive in the evolutionary struggle. This is sometimes called the natural selection theory of knowledge and holds that ideas have 'survival value' and that knowledge evolves through a process of variation, selection and retention. They have adaptive value and are probably as close as our species can come to being objective and understanding reality.

VALIDITY

The first thing we have to ask is: "validity of what?" When we think about validity in research, most of us think about research components. We might say that a measure is a valid one, or that a valid sample was drawn, or that the design had strong validity. But all of those statements are technically incorrect. Measures, samples and designs don't 'have' validity—only propositions can be said to be valid. Technically, we should say that a measure leads to valid conclusions or that a sample enables valid inferences, and so on. It is a proposition, inference or conclusion that can 'have' validity.

We make lots of different inferences or conclusions while conducting research. Many of these are related to the process of doing research and are not the major hypotheses of the study. Nevertheless, like the bricks that go into building a wall, these intermediate process and methodological propositions provide the foundation for the substantive conclusions that we wish to address. For instance, virtually all social research involves measurement or observation. And, whenever we measure or observe we are concerned with whether we are measuring what we intend to measure or with how our observations are influenced by the circumstances in which they are made.

We reach conclusions about the quality of our measures—conclusions that will play an important role in addressing the broader substantive issues of our study. When we talk about the validity of research, we are often referring to these to the many conclusions we reach about the quality of different parts of our research methodology. We subdivide validity into four types. Each type addresses a specific methodological question. In order to understand the types of validity, you have to know something about how we investigate a research question. Because all four validity types are really only operative when studying causal questions, we will use a causal study to set the context.

There are really two realms that are involved in research. The first, on the top, is the land of theory. It is what goes on inside our heads as researchers. It is were we keep our theories about how the world operates. The second, on the bottom, is the land of observations. It is the real world into which we translate our ideas—our programmes, treatments, measures and observations. When we conduct research, we are continually flitting back and forth between these two realms, between what we think about the world and what is going on in it.

When we are investigating a cause-effect relationship, we have a theory (implicit or otherwise) of what the cause is (the cause construct). For instance, if we are testing a new educational programme, we have an idea of what it would look like ideally. Similarly, on the effect side, we have an idea of what we are ideally trying to affect and measure (the effect construct). But each of these, the cause and the effect, has to be translated into real things, into a programme or treatment and a measure or observational method. We use the term operationalisation to describe the act of translating a construct into its manifestation.

In effect, we take our idea and describe it as a series of operations or procedures. Now, instead of it only being an idea in our minds, it becomes a public entity that anyone can look at and examine for themselves. It is one thing, for instance, for you to say that you would like to measure self-esteem (a construct). But when you show a ten-item paper-and-pencil self-esteem measure that you developed for that purpose, others can look at it and understand more clearly what you intend by the term self-esteem.

For any inference or conclusion, there are always possible threats to validity—reasons the conclusion or inference might be wrong. Ideally, one tries to reduce the plausibility of the most likely threats to validity, thereby leaving as most plausible the conclusion reached in the study. For instance, imagine a study examining whether there is a relationship between the amount of training in a specific technology and subsequent rates of use of that technology. Because the interest is in a relationship, it is considered an issue of conclusion validity. Assume that the study is completed and no significant correlation between amount of training and adoption rates is found.

On this basis it is concluded that there is no relationship between the two. For one, it's possible that there isn't sufficient statistical power to detect a relationship even if it exists. Perhaps the sample size is too small or the measure of amount of training is unreliable. Or maybe assumptions of the correlational test are violated given the variables used. Perhaps there were random irrelevancies in the study setting or random heterogeneity in the respondents that increased the variability in the data and made it harder to see the relationship of interest.

The inference that there is no relationship will be stronger—have greater conclusion validity—if one can show that these alternative explanations are not credible. The distributions might be examined to see if they conform with assumptions of the statistical test, or analyses conducted to determine whether there is sufficient statistical power. The theory of validity, and the many lists of specific threats, provide a useful scheme for assessing the quality of research conclusions. The theory is general in scope and applicability, well-articulated in its philosophical suppositions, and virtually impossible to explain adequately in a few minutes. As a framework for judging the quality of evaluations it is indispensable and well worth understanding.

ETHICAL PRINCIPLES

We are going through a time of profound change in our understanding of the ethics of applied social research. From the time immediately after World War II until the early 1990s, there was a gradually developing consensus about the key ethical principles that should underlie the research endeavour. Two marker events stand out as symbolic of this consensus. The Nuremberg War Crimes Trial following World War II brought to public view the ways German scientists had used captive human subjects as subjects in oftentimes gruesome experiments.

In the 1950s and 1960s, the Tuskegee Syphilis Study involved the withholding of known effective treatment for syphilis from African-American participants who were infected. Events like these forced the reexamination of ethical standards and the gradual development of a consensus that potential human subjects needed to be protected from being used as 'guinea pigs' in scientific research. By the 1990s, the dynamics of the situation changed. Cancer patients and persons with AIDS fought publicly with the medical research establishment about the long time needed to get approval for and complete research into potential cures for fatal diseases.

In many cases, it is the ethical assumptions of the previous thirty years that drive this 'go-slow' mentality. After all, we would rather risk denying treatment for a while until we achieve enough confidence in a treatment, rather than run the risk of harming innocent people. But now, those who were threatened with fatal illness were saying to the research establishment that they *wanted* to be test subjects, even under experimental conditions of considerable risk. You had several very vocal and articulate patient groups who wanted to be experimented on coming up against an ethical review system that was designed to protect them from being experimented on.

Although the last few years in the ethics of research have been tumultuous ones, it is beginning to appear that a new consensus is evolving that involves the stakeholder groups most affected by a problem participating more actively in the formulation of guidelines for research. While it's not entirely clear, at present, what the new consensus will be, it is almost certain that it will not fall at either extreme: protecting against human experimentation at all costs vs. allowing anyone who is willing to be experimented on. There are a number of key phrases that describe the system of ethical protections that the contemporary social and medical research establishment have created to try to protect better the rights of their research participants.

The principle of voluntary participation requires that people not be coerced into participating in research. This is especially relevant where researchers had previously relied on 'captive audiences' for their subjects—prisons, universities, and places like that. Closely related to the notion of voluntary participation is the requirement of informed consent. Essentially, this means that prospective research participants must be fully informed about the procedures and risks involved in research and must give their consent to participate.

Ethical standards also require that researchers not put participants in a situation where they might be at *risk of* harm as a result of their participation. Harm can be defined as both physical and psychological. There are two standards that are applied in order to help protect the privacy of research participants. Almost all research guarantees the participants confidentiality—they are assured that identifying information will not be made available to anyone who is not directly involved in the study. The stricter standard is the principle of anonymity which essentially means that the participant will remain anonymous throughout the study—even to the researchers themselves.

Clearly, the anonymity standard is a stronger guarantee of privacy, but it is sometimes difficult to accomplish, especially in situations where participants have to be measured at multiple time points. Increasingly, researchers have had to deal with the ethical issue of a person's right to service. Good research practice often requires the use of a no-treatment control group—a group of participants who do not get the treatment or programme that is being studied. But when that treatment or programme may have beneficial effects, persons assigned to the no-treatment control may feel their rights to equal access to services are being curtailed. Even when clear ethical standards and principles exist, there will be times when the need to do accurate research runs up against the rights of potential participants. No set of standards can possibly anticipate every ethical circumstance.

Furthermore, there needs to be a procedure that assures that researchers will consider all relevant ethical issues in formulating research plans. To address such needs most institutions and organisations have formulated an Institutional Review Board (IRB), a panel of persons who reviews grant proposals with respect to ethical implications and decides whether additional actions need to be taken to assure the safety and rights of participants. By reviewing proposals for research, IRBs also help to protect both the organisation and the researcher against potential legal implications of neglecting to address important ethical issues of participants.

3

Research Design

Research design provides the glue that holds the research project together. A design is used to structure the research, to show how all of the major parts of the research project—the samples or groups, measures, treatments or programmes, and methods of assignment—work together to try to address the central research questions. Research design can be thought of as the structure of research—it is the "glue" that holds all of the elements in a research project together. We often describe a design using a concise notation that enables us to summarise a complex design structure efficiently. What are the "elements" that a design includes? They are:

— *Observations or Measures*: These are symbolised by an 'O' in design notation. An O can refer to a single measure, a single instrument with multiple items, a complex multi-part instrument, or a whole battery of tests or measures given out on one occasion. If you need to distinguish among specific measures, you can use subscripts with the O, as in O1, O2, and so on.

— *Treatments or Programmes*: These are symbolised with an 'X' in design notations. The X can refer to a simple intervention or to a complex hodgepodge programme. Usually, a no-treatment control or comparison group has no symbol for the treatment (some researchers use X+ and X- to indicate the treatment and control respectively). As with observations, you can use subscripts to distinguish different programmes or programme variations.

— *Groups*: Each group in a design is given its own line in the design structure, if the design notation has three lines, there are three groups in the design.

— *Assignment to Group*: Assignment to group is designated by a letter at the beginning of each line that describes how the group was assigned. The major types of assignment are:

  — R = random assignment.

  — N = nonequivalent groups.

  — C = assignment by cutoff.

  — Time.

  Time moves from left to right. Elements that are listed on the left occur before elements that are listed on the right.

TYPES OF RESEARCH DESIGNS

We can classify designs into a simple threefold classification by asking some key questions. First, does the design use random assignment to groups? If random assignment is used, we call the design a randomised experiment or true experiment. If random assignment is not used, then we have to ask a second question: Does the design use either multiple groups or multiple waves of measurement? If the answer is yes, we would label it a quasi-experimental design. If no, we would call it a non-experimental design. This threefold classification is especially useful for describing the design with respect to internal validity.

A randomised experiment generally is the strongest of the three designs when your interest is in establishing a cause-effect relationship. A non-experiment is generally the weakest in this respect. To illustrate the different types of designs, consider one of each in design notation. The first design is a posttest-only randomised experiment. You can tell it's a randomised experiment because it has an R at the beginning of each line, indicating random assignment. The second design is a pre-post nonequivalent groups quasi-experiment.

We know it's not a randomised experiment because random assignment wasn't used. And we know it's not a non-experiment because there are both multiple groups and multiple waves of measurement. That means it must be a quasi-experiment. We add the label "nonequivalent" because in this design we do not explicitly control the assignment and the groups may be nonequivalent or not similar to each other.

Finally, we show a posttest-only nonexperimental design. You might use this design if you want to study the effects of a natural disaster like a flood or tornado and you want to do so by interviewing survivors. Notice that in this design, you don't have a comparison group and you don't have multiple waves of measurement. Does it make sense to do the non-experimental study? Of course! You could gain lots of valuable information by well-conducted post-disaster interviews. But you may have a hard time establishing which of the things you observed are due to the disaster rather than to other factors like the peculiarities of the town or pre-disaster characteristics.

Experimental Design

Experimental designs are often touted as the most "rigorous" of all research designs or, as the "gold standard" against which all other designs are judged. In one sense, they probably are. If you can implement an experimental design well, then the experiment is probably the strongest design with respect to internal validity. Why? Recall that internal validity is at the centre of all causal or cause-effect inferences. When you want to determine whether some programme or treatment causes some outcome or outcomes to occur, then you are interested in having strong internal validity. Essentially, you want to assess the proposition:

If X, then Y

or, in more colloquial terms:

If the programme is given, then the outcome occurs.

Unfortunately, it's not enough just to show that when the programme or treatment occurs the expected outcome also happens. That's because there may be lots of reasons, other than the programme, for why you observed the outcome. To really show that there is a causal relationship, you have to simultaneously address the two propositions:

If X, then Y

and

If *not* X, then *not* Y

Or, once again more colloquially:

If the programme is given, then the outcome occurs.

and

If the programme is *not* given, then the outcome does *not* occur.

If you are able to provide evidence for both of these propositions, then you've in effect isolated the programme from all of the other potential causes of the outcome. You've shown that when the programme is present the outcome occurs and when it's not present, the outcome doesn't occur. That points to the causal effectiveness of the programme.

Think of all this like a fork in the road. Down one path, you implement the programme and observe the outcome. Down the other path, you don't implement the programme and the outcome doesn't occur. But, how do we take both paths in the road in the same study? How can we be in two places at once? Ideally, what we want is to have the same conditions—the same people, context, time, and so on—and see whether when the programme is given we get the outcome and when the programme is not given we don't.

Obviously, we can never achieve this hypothetical situation. If we give the programme to a group of people, we can't simultaneously not give it! So, how do we get out of this apparent dilemma? Perhaps we just need to think about the problem a little differently. What if we could create two groups or contexts that are as similar as we can possibly make them? If we could be confident that the two situations are comparable, then we could administer our programme in one and not give the programme in the other. And, if the two contexts are comparable, then this is like taking both forks in the road simultaneously! We can have our cake and eat it too, so to speak.

That's exactly what an experimental design tries to achieve. In the simplest type of experiment, we create two groups that are "equivalent" to each other. One group (the programme or treatment group) gets the programme and the other group (the comparison or control group) does not. In all other respects, the groups are treated the same. They have similar people, live in similar contexts, have similar backgrounds, and so on. Now, if we observe differences in outcomes between these two groups, then the differences must be due to the only thing that differs between them—that one got the programme and the other didn't.

So how do we create two groups that are "equivalent"? The approach used in experimental design is to assign people randomly from a common pool of people into the two groups. The experiment relies on this idea of random assignment to groups as the basis for obtaining two groups that are similar. Then, we give one the programme or treatment and we don't give it to the other. We observe the same outcomes in both groups. The key to the success of the experiment is in the random assignment.

In fact, even with random assignment we never expect that the groups we create will be exactly the same. How could they be, when they are made up of different people? We rely on the idea of probability and assume that the two groups are "probabilistically equivalent" or equivalent within known probabilistic ranges. So, if we randomly assign people to two groups, and we have enough people in our study to achieve the desired probabilistic equivalence, then we may consider the experiment to be strong in internal validity and we probably have a good shot at assessing whether the programme causes the outcome(s).

But there are lots of things that can go wrong. We may not have a large enough sample. Or, we may have people who refuse to participate in our study or who drop out part way through. Or, we may be challenged successfully on ethical grounds. Or, we may get resistance from the staff in our study who would like some of their "favourite" people to get the programme. Or, they may or might insist that her daughter be put into the new programme in an educational study because it may mean she'll get better grades.

The bottom line here is that experimental design is intrusive and difficult to carry out in most real world contexts. And, because an experiment is often an intrusion, you are to some extent setting up an artificial situation so that you can assess your causal relationship with high internal validity. If so, then you are limiting the degree to which you can generalise your results to real contexts where you haven't set up an experiment.

That is, you have reduced your external validity in order to achieve greater internal validity. In the end, there is just no simple answer. If the situation is right, an experiment can be a very strong design to use. But it isn't automatically so. Experimental design is a fairly complex subject in its own right. There are lots of experimental design variations that attempt to accomplish different things or solve different problems. In this section you'll explore the basic design and then learn some of the principles behind the major variations.

Two-Group Experimental Designs

The simplest of all experimental designs is the two-group posttest-only randomised experiment. In design notation, it has two lines—one for each group—with an R at the beginning of each line to indicate that the groups were randomly assigned. One group gets the treatment or programme (the X) and the other group is the comparison group and doesn't get the programme.

Notice that a pretest is not required for this design. Usually we include a pretest in order to determine whether groups are comparable prior to the programme, but because we are using random assignment we can assume that the two groups are probabilistically equivalent to begin with and the pretest is not required.

In this design, we are most interested in determining whether the two groups are different after the programme.

Typically we measure the groups on one or more measures (the Os in notation) and we compare them by testing for the differences between the means using a t-test or one way Analysis of Variance (ANOVA). The posttest-only randomised experiment is strong against the single-group threats to internal validity because it's not a single group design! It's strong against the all of the multiple-group threats except for selection-mortality. For instance, it's strong against selection-testing and selection-instrumentation because it doesn't use repeated measurement.

The selection-mortality threat is especially salient if there are differential rates of dropouts in the two groups. This could result if the treatment or programme is a noxious or negative one or if the control group condition is painful or intolerable. This design is susceptible to all of the social interaction threats to internal validity. Because the design requires random assignment, in some institutional settings it is more likely to utilise persons who would be aware of each other and of the conditions they've been assigned to.

The posttest-only randomised experimental design is, despite its simple structure, one of the best research designs for assessing cause-effect relationships. It is easy to execute and, because it uses only a posttest, is relatively inexpensive. But there are many variations on this simple experimental design. You can begin to explore these by looking at how we classify the various experimental designs.

Probabilistic Equivalence

What do we mean by the term probabilistic equivalence?

Well, to begin with, we certainly don't mean that two groups are equal to each other. When we deal with human beings it is impossible to ever say that any two individuals or groups are equal or equivalent.

Clearly the important term in the phrase is "probabilistic". This means that the type of equivalence we have is based on the notion of probabilities. In more concrete terms, probabilistic equivalence means that we know perfectly the odds that we will find a difference between two groups. Notice, it doesn't mean that the means of the two groups will be equal. It just means that we know the odds that they won't be equal.

We achieve probabilistic equivalence through the mechanism of random assignment to groups. When we randomly assign to groups, we can calculate the chance that the two groups will differ just because of the random assignment. Let's say we are assigning a group of first grade students to two groups. Further, let's assume that the average test scores for these children for a standardised test with a population mean of 50 were 49 and 51 respectively. We might conduct a t-test to see if the means of our two randomly assigned groups are statistically different.

We know—through random assignment and the law of large numbers—that the chance that they will be different is 5 out of 100 when we set our significance level to .05. In other words, 5 times out of every 100, when we randomly assign two groups, we can expect to get a significant difference at the .05 level of significance. When we assign randomly, the only reason the groups can differ is because of chance assignment because their assignment is entirely based on the randomness of assignment.

If, by chance, the groups differ on one variable, we have no reason to believe that they will automatically be different on any other. Even if we find that the groups differ on a pretest, we have no reason to suspect that they will differ on a posttest. Why? Because their pretest difference had to be a chance one. So, when we randomly assign, we are able to assume that the groups do have a form of equivalence. We don't expect them to be equal. But we do expect that they are "probabilistically" equal.

Random Selection and Assignment

Random selection is how you draw the sample of people for your study from a population. Random assignment is how you assign the sample that you draw to different groups or treatments in your study. It is possible to have both random selection and assignment in a study. Let's say you drew a random sample of 100 clients from a population list of 1000 current clients of your organisation. That is random sampling. Now, let's say you randomly assign 50 of these clients to get some new additional treatment and the other 50 to be controls. That's random assignment.

It is also possible to have only one of these (random selection or random assignment) but not the other in a study. For instance, if you do not randomly draw the 100 cases from your list of 1000 but instead just take the first 100 on the list, you do not have random selection. But you could still randomly assign this nonrandom sample to treatment versus control. Or, you could randomly select 100 from your list of 1000 and then nonrandomly assign them to treatment or control.

And, it's possible to have neither random selection nor random assignment. In a typical nonequivalent groups design in education you might nonrandomly choose two 5th grade classes to be in your study. This is nonrandom selection. Then, you could arbitrarily assign one to get the new educational programme and the other to be the control. This is nonrandom assignment. Random selection is related to sampling. Therefore it is most related to the external validity of your results. After all, we would randomly sample so that our research participants better represent the larger group from which they're drawn.

Random assignment is most related to design. In fact, when we randomly assign participants to treatments we have, by definition, an experimental design. Therefore, random assignment is most related to internal validity. After all, we randomly assign in order to help assure that our treatment groups are similar to each other prior to the treatment.

Variety of Experimental Designs

Although there are a great variety of experimental design variations, we can classify and organise them using a simple signal-to-noise ratio metaphor. In this metaphor, we assume that what we observe or see can be divided into two components, the signal and the noise. The figure, for instance, shows a time series with a slightly downward slope. But because there is so much variability or noise in the series, it is difficult even to detect the downward slope. When we divide the series into its two components, we can clearly see the slope.

In most research, the signal is related to the key variable of interest—the construct you're trying to measure, the programme or treatment that's being implemented. The noise consists of all of the random factors in the situation that make it harder to see the signal—the lighting in the room, local distractions, how people felt that day, etc. We can construct a ratio of these two by dividing the signal by the noise. In research, we want the signal to be high relative to the noise. For instance, if you have a very powerful treatment or programme and very good measurement you will have a better chance of seeing the effect of the programme than if you have either a strong programme and weak measurement or a weak programme and strong measurement.

With this in mind, we can now classify the experimental designs into two categories: signal enhancers or noise reducers. Notice that doing either of these things—enhancing signal or reducing noise—improves the quality of the research. The signal-enhancing experimental designs are called the factorial designs. In these designs, the focus is almost entirely on the setup of the programme or treatment, its components and its major dimensions.

In a typical factorial design we would examine a number of different variations of a treatment. There are two major types of noise-reducing experimental designs: covariance designs and blocking designs. In these designs we typically use information about the makeup of the sample or about pre-programme variables to remove some of the noise in our study.

Factorial Designs

Factorial design is an experiment whose design consists of two or more factors, each with discrete possible values or "levels", and whose experimental units take on all possible combinations of these levels across all such factors. Such an experiment allows studying the effect of each factor on the response variable, as well as the effects of interactions between factors on the response variable.

For the vast majority of factorial experiments, each factor has only two levels. If the number of experiments for a full factorial design is too high to be logistically feasible, a fractional factorial design may be done, in which some of the possible combinations are omitted.

Factorial designs were used in the 19th century by John Bennet Lawes and Joseph Henry Gilbert of the Rothamsted Experimental Station. Ronald Fisher argued in 1926 that "complex" designs were more efficient than studying one factor at a time. Fisher wrote, "No aphorism is more frequently repeated in connection with field trials, than that we must ask Nature few questions, or, ideally, one question, at a time.

The writer is convinced that this view is wholly mistaken. Nature, he suggests, will best respond to a logical and carefully thought out questionnaire". A factorial design allows the effect of several factors and even interactions between them to be determined with the same number of trials as are necessary to determine any one of the effects by itself with the same degree of accuracy. The simplest factorial experiment contains two levels for each of two factors. Suppose an engineer wishes to study the total power used by each of two different motors, A and B, running at each of two different speeds, 2000 or 3000 RPM.

The factorial experiment would consist of four experimental units: motor A at 2000 RPM, motor B at 2000 RPM, motor A at 3000 RPM, and motor B at 3000 RPM. Each combination of a single level selected from every factor is present once. This experiment is an example of a 22 (or 2x2) factorial experiment, so named because it considers two levels (the base) for each of two factors (the power or superscript), producing 22=4 factorial points.

Designs can involve many independent variables. As a further example, the effects of three input variables can be evaluated in eight experimental conditions shown as the corners of a cube. This can be conducted with or without replication, depending on its intended purpose and available resources. It will provide the effects of the three independent variables on the dependent variable and possible interactions. A factorial experiment can be analysed using ANOVA or regression analysis. It is relatively easy to estimate the main effect for a factor.

To compute the main effect of a factor "A", subtract the average response of all experimental runs for which A was at its low (or first) level from the average response of all experimental runs for which A was at its high (or second) level. Other useful exploratory analysis tools for factorial experiments include main effects plots, interaction plots, and a normal probability plot of the estimated effects. When the factors are continuous, two-level factorial designs assume that the effects are linear. If a quadratic effect is expected for a factor, a more complicated experiment should be used, such as a central composite design. Optimisation of factors that could have quadratic effects is the primary goal of response surface methodology.

It's clear that factorial designs can become cumbersome and have too many groups even with only a few factors. In much research, you won't be interested in a fully-crossed factorial design like the ones we've been showing that pair every combination of levels of factors. Some of the combinations may not make sense from a policy or administrative perspective, or you simply may not have enough funds to implement all combinations. In this case, you may decide to implement an incomplete factorial design.

In this variation, some of the cells are intentionally left empty—you don't assign people to get those combinations of factors. One of the most common uses of incomplete factorial design is to allow for a control or placebo group that receives no treatment. In this case, it is actually impossible to implement a group that simultaneously has several levels of treatment factors and receives no treatment at all. So, we consider the control group to be its own cell in an incomplete factorial rubric.

This allows us to conduct both relative and absolute treatment comparisons within a single study and to get a fairly precise look at different treatment combinations.

Randomised Block Designs

The Randomised Block Design is research design's equivalent to stratified random sampling. Like stratified sampling, randomised block designs are constructed to reduce noise or variance in the data. How do they do it? They require that the researcher divide the sample into relatively homogeneous subgroups or blocks. Then, the experimental design you want to implement is implemented within each block or homogeneous subgroup. The key idea is that the variability within each block is less than the variability of the entire sample.

Thus each estimate of the treatment effect within a block is more efficient than estimates across the entire sample. And, when we pool these more efficient estimates across blocks, we should get an overall more efficient estimate than we would without blocking. Here, we can see a simple example. Let's assume that we originally intended to conduct a simple posttest-only randomised experimental design. But, we recognise that our sample has several intact or homogeneous subgroups. For instance, in a study of college students, we might expect that students are relatively homogeneous with respect to class or year. So, we decide to block the sample into four groups: freshman, sophomore, junior, and senior.

If our hunch is correct, that the variability within class is less than the variability for the entire sample, we will probably get more powerful estimates of the treatment effect within each block. Within each of our four blocks, we would implement the simple post-only randomised experiment. Notice a couple of things about this strategy.

First, to an external observer, it may not be apparent that you are blocking. You would be implementing the same design in each block. And, there is no reason that the people in different blocks need to be segregated or separated from each other.

In other words, blocking doesn't necessarily affect anything that you do with the research participants. Instead, blocking is a strategy for grouping people in your data analysis in order to reduce noise—it is an analysis strategy. Second, you will only benefit from a blocking design if you are correct in your hunch that the blocks are more homogeneous than the entire sample is. If you are wrong—if different college-level classes aren't relatively homogeneous with respect to your measures—you will actually be hurt by blocking.

You need to consider carefully whether the groups are relatively homogeneous. If you are measuring political attitudes, for instance, is it reasonable to believe that freshmen are more like each other than they are like sophomores or juniors? Would they be more homogeneous with respect to measures related to drug abuse? Ultimately the decision to block involves judgment on the part of the researcher.

Analysis of Covariance Designs

The basic Analysis of Covariance Design (ANCOVA or ANACOVA) is a just pretest-posttest randomised experimental design. The notation shown here suggests that the pre-programme measure is the same one as the post-programme measure, and so we would call this a pretest. But you should note that the pre-programme measure doesn't have to be a pretest—it can be any variable measured prior to the programme intervention. It is also possible for a study to have more than one covariate.

The pre-programme measure or pretest is sometimes also called a "covariate" because of the way it's used in the data analysis—we "covary" it with the outcome variable or posttest in order to remove variability or noise. Thus, the ANCOVA design falls in the class of a "noise reduction" experimental design. In social research we frequently hear about statistical "adjustments" that attempt to control for important factors in our study. For instance, we might read that an analysis "examined post-test performance after adjusting for the income and educational level of the participants."

In this case, "income" and "education level" are covariates. Covariates are the variables you "adjust for" in your study. Sometimes the language that will be used is that of "removing the effects" of one variable from another. For instance, we might read that an analysis "examined posttest performance after removing the effect of income and educational level of the participants." One of the most important ideas in social research is how we make a statistical adjustment—adjust one variable based on its covariance with another variable. If you understand this idea, you'll be well on your way to mastering social research.

Hybrid Experimental Designs

Hybrid experimental designs are just what the name implies—new strains that are formed by combining features of more established designs. There are lots of variations that could be constructed from standard design features. Here, we are going to introduce two hybrid designs.

Solomon Four-Group Design

The Solomon Four-Group Design is designed to deal with a potential testing threat. Recall that a testing threat occurs when the act of taking a test affects how people score on a retest or post-test. It's probably not a big surprise that this design has four groups. Note that two of the groups receive the treatment and two do not. Further, two of the groups receive a pretest and two do not. One way to view this is as a 2x2 (Treatment Group X Measurement Group) factorial design. Within each treatment condition we have a group that is pretested and one that is not. By explicitly including testing as a factor in the design, we are able to assess experimentally whether a testing threat is operating.

Possible Outcomes: Let's look at a couple of possible outcomes from this design. The first outcome graph shows what the data might look like if there is a treatment or programme effect and there is no testing threat. You need to be careful in interpreting this graph to note that there are six dots—one to represent the average for each O in the design notation. To help you visually see the connection between the pretest and posttest average for the same group, a line is used to connect the dots.

The two dots that are not connected by a line represent the two post-only groups. Look first at the two pretest means. They are close to each because the groups were randomly assigned. On the posttest, both treatment groups outscored both controls. Now, look at the post-test values. There appears to be no difference between the treatment groups, even though one got a pretest and the other did not. Similarly, the two control groups scored about the same on the post-test. Thus, the pretest did not appear to affect the outcome. But both treatment groups clearly outscored both controls. There is a main effect for the treatment.

Now, look at a result where there is evidence of a testing threat. In this outcome, the pretests are again equivalent. Each treatment group outscored it's comparable control group. The pre-post treatment outscored the pre-post control. And, the post-only treatment outscored the post-only control. These results indicate that there is a treatment effect. But here, both groups that had the pretest outscored their comparable non-pretest group. That's evidence for a testing threat.

Switching Replications

The Switching Replications design is one of the strongest of the experimental designs. And, when the circumstances are right for this design, it addresses one of the major problems in experimental designs—the need to deny the programme to some participants through random assignment. The design notation indicates that this is a two group design with three waves of measurement. You might think of this as two pre-post treatment-control designs grafted together. That is, the implementation of the treatment is repeated or replicated.

And in the repetition of the treatment, the two groups switch roles—the original control group becomes the treatment group in phase 2 while the original treatment acts as the control. By the end of the study all participants have received the treatment. The switching replications design is most feasible in organisational contexts where programmes are repeated at regular intervals. For instance, it works especially well in schools that are on a semester system. All students are pretested at the beginning of the school year.

During the first semester, Group 1 receives the treatment and during the second semester Group 2 gets it. The design also enhances organisational efficiency in resource allocation. Schools only need to allocate enough resources to give the programme to half of the students at a time.

Possible Outcomes: Let's look at two possible outcomes. In the first example, we see that when the programme is given to the first group, the recipients do better than the controls. In the second phase, when the programme is given to the original controls, they "catch up" to the original programme group. Thus, we have a converge, diverge, reconverge outcome pattern. We might expect a result like this when the programme covers specific content that the students master in the short-term and where we don't expect that they will continue getting better as a result.

Now, look at the other example result. During the first phase we see the same result as before—the programme group improves while the control does not. And, as before, during the second phase we see the original control group, now the programme group, improve as much as did the first programme group. But now, during phase two, the original programme group continues to increase even though the programme is no longer being given them. It could happen in circumstances where the programme has continuing and longer term effects. For instance, if the programme focused on learning skills, students might continue to improve even after the formal programme period because they continue to apply the skills and improve in them.

Quasi-Experimental Design

A quasi-experimental design is one that looks a bit like an experimental design but lacks the key ingredient—random assignment. With respect to internal validity, they often appear to be inferior to randomised experiments. But there is something compelling about these designs; taken as a group, they are easily more frequently implemented than their randomised cousins.

Probably the most commonly used quasi-experimental design is the nonequivalent groups design.

In its simplest form it requires a pretest and post-test for a treated and comparison group. It's identical to the Analysis of Covariance design except that the groups are not created through random assignment. You will see that the lack of random assignment, and the potential nonequivalence between the groups, complicates the statistical analysis of the nonequivalent groups design. There is one major class of quasi-experimental designs that are not included here—the interrupted time series designs.

Nonequivalent Groups Design (NEGD)

The Non-Equivalent Groups Design is probably the most frequently used design in social research. It is structured like a pretest-posttest randomised experiment, but it lacks the key feature of the randomised designs—random assignment. In the NEGD, we most often use intact groups that we think are similar as the treatment and control groups. In education, we might pick two comparable classrooms or schools. In community-based research, we might use two similar communities.

We try to select groups that are as similar as possible so we can fairly compare the treated one with the comparison one. But we can never be sure the groups are comparable. Or, put another way, it's unlikely that the two groups would be as similar as they would if we assigned them through a random lottery. Because it's often likely that the groups are not equivalent, this designed was named the nonequivalent groups design to remind us.

So, what does the term "nonequivalent" mean? In one sense, it just means that assignment to group was not random. In other words, the researcher did not control the assignment to groups through the mechanism of random assignment. As a result, the groups may be different prior to the study. That is, the NEGD is especially susceptible to the internal validity threat of selection. Any prior differences between the groups may affect the outcome of the study. Under the worst circumstances, this can lead us to conclude that our programme didn't make a difference when in fact it did, or that it did make a difference when in fact it didn't.

Regression-Discontinuity (RD) Design

In everyday language both parts of the term have connotations that are primarily negative. To most people "regression" implies a reversion backwards or a return to some earlier, more primitive state while "discontinuity" suggests an unnatural jump or shift in what might otherwise be a smoother, more continuous process. To a research methodologist, however, the term regression-discontinuity carries no such negative meaning. Instead, the RD design is seen as a useful method for determining whether a programme or treatment is effective.

The label "RD design" actually refers to a set of design variations. In its simplest most traditional form, the RD design is a pretest-posttest programme-comparison group strategy. The unique characteristic which sets RD designs apart from other pre-post group designs is the method by which research participants are assigned to conditions. In RD designs, participants are assigned to programme or comparison groups solely on the basis of a cutoff score on a pre-programme measure. Thus the RD design is distinguished from randomised experiments and from other quasi-experimental strategies by its unique method of assignment.

This cutoff criterion implies the major advantage of RD designs—they are appropriate when we wish to target a programme or treatment to those who most need or deserve it. Thus, unlike its randomised or quasi-experimental alternatives, the RD design does not require us to assign potentially needy individuals to a no-programme comparison group in order to evaluate the effectiveness of a programme. The RD design has not been used frequently in social research. The most common implementation has been in compensatory education evaluation where school children who obtain scores which fall below some predetermined cutoff value on an achievement test are assigned to remedial training designed to improve their performance.

The low frequency of use may be attributable to several factors. Certainly, the design is a relative latecomer. Its first major field tests did not occur until the mid-1970s when it was incorporated into the nationwide evaluation system for compensatory education programmes funded under Title I of the Elementary and Secondary Education Act (ESEA) of 1965. In many situations, the design has not been used because one or more key criteria were absent. For instance, RD designs force administrators to assign participants to conditions solely on the basis of quantitative indicators thereby often impalatably restricting the degree to which judgment, discretion or favoritism may be used.

Perhaps the most telling reason for the lack of wider adoption of the RD design is that at first glance the design doesn't seem to make sense. In most research, we wish to have comparison groups that are equivalent to programme groups on pre-programme indicators so that post-programme differences may be attributed to the programme itself. But because of the cutoff criterion in RD designs, programme and comparison groups are deliberately and maximally different on pre-programme characteristics, an apparently insensible anomaly.

An understanding of how the design actually works depends on at least a conceptual familiarity with regression analysis thereby making the strategy a difficult one to convey to nonstatistical audiences. Despite its lack of use, the RD design has great potential for evaluation and programme research. From a methodological point of view, inferences which are drawn from a well-implemented RD design are comparable in internal validity to conclusions from randomised experiments. Thus, the RD design is a strong competitor to randomised designs when causal hypotheses are being investigated.

From an ethical perspective, RD designs are compatible with the goal of getting the programme to those most in need. It is not necessary to deny the programme from potentially deserving recipients simply for the sake of a scientific test. From an administrative viewpoint, the RD design is often directly usable with existing measurement efforts such as the regularly collected statistical information typical of most management information systems. The advantages of the RD design warrant greater educational efforts on the part of the methodological community to encourage its use where appropriate.

The "basic" RD design is a pretest-posttest two group design. The term "pretest- posttest" implies that the same measure is administered before and after some programme or treatment. The term "pretest" implies that the same measure is given twice while the term "pre-programme" measure implies more broadly that before and after measures may be the same or different. It is assumed that a cutoff value on the pretest or pre-programme measure is being used to assign persons or other units to the programme. Two group versions of the RD design might imply either that some treatment or programme is being contrasted with a no-programme condition or that two alternative programmes are being compared.

The description of the basic design as a two group design implies that a single pretest cutoff score is used to assign participants to either the programme or comparison group. The term "participants" refers to whatever unit is assigned. In many cases, participants are individuals, but they could be any definable units such as hospital wards, hospitals, counties, and so on. To make this initial presentation more concrete, we can imagine a hypothetical study where the interest is in examining the effect of a new treatment protocol for inpatients with a particular diagnosis.

For simplicity, we can assume that we wish to try the new protocol on patients who are considered most ill and that for each patient we have a continuous quantitative indicator of health that is a composite rating which can take values from 1 to 100 where high scores indicate greater health. Furthermore, we can assume that a pretest cutoff score of 50 was chosen as the assignment criterion or that all those scoring lower than 50 on the pretest are to be given the new treatment protocol while those with scores greater than or equal to 50 are given the standard treatment.

Selection of the Cutoff: The choice of cutoff value is usually based on one of two factors. It can be made solely on the basis of the programme resources that are available. For instance, if a programme only has the capability of handling 25 persons and 70 people apply, one can choose a cutoff point that distinguishes the 25 most needy persons from the rest. Alternatively, the cutoff can be chosen on substantive grounds. If the pre-programme assignment measure is an indication of severity of illness measured on a 1 to 7 scale and physicians or other experts believe that all patients scoring 5 or more are critical and fit well the criteria defined for programme participants then a cutoff value of 5 may be used.

Interpretation of Results: In order to interpret the results of an RD design, one must know the nature of the assignment variable, who received the programme and the nature of the outcome measure. Without this information, there is no distinct outcome pattern which directly indicates whether an effect is positive or negative.

To illustrate this, we can construct a new hypothetical example of an RD design. Let us assume that a hospital administrator would like to improve the quality of patient care through the institution of an intensive quality of care training programme for staff. Because of financial constraints, the programme is too costly to implement for all employees and so instead it will be administered to the entire staff from specifically targeted units or wards which seem most in need of improving quality of care.

Two general measures of quality of care are available. The first is an aggregate rating of quality of care based on observation and rating by an administrative staff member and will be labelled here the QOC rating. The second is the ratio of the number of recorded patient complaints relative to the number of patients in the unit over a fixed period of time and will be termed here the Complaint Ratio. In this scenario, the administrator could use either the QOC rating or Complaint Ratio as the basis for assigning units to receive the training. Similarly, the effects of the training could be measured on either variable.

The Role of the Comparison Group in RD Designs: With this introductory discussion of the design in mind, we can now see what constitutes the benchmark for comparison in the RD design. In experimental or other quasi- experimental designs we either assume or try to provide evidence that the programme and comparison groups are equivalent prior to the programme so that post-programme differences can be attributed to the manipulation.

The RD design involves no such assumption. Instead, with RD designs we assume that in the absence of the programme the pre-post relationship would be equivalent for the two groups. Thus, the strength of the RD design is dependent on two major factors. The first is the assumption that there is no spurious discontinuity in the pre-post relationship which happens to coincide with the cutoff point. The second factor concerns the degree to which we can know and correctly model the pre-post relationship and constitutes the major problem in the statistical analysis of the RD design which will be discussed below.

The Internal Validity of the RD Design: Internal validity refers to whether one can infer that the treatment or programme being investigated caused a change in outcome indicators. Internal validity as conceived is not concerned with our ability to generalise but rather focuses on whether a causal relationship can be demonstrated for the immediate research context. Research designs which address causal questions are often compared on their relative ability to yield internally valid results.

In most causal hypothesis tests, the central inferential question is whether any observed outcome differences between groups are attributable to the programme or instead to some other factor. In order to argue for the internal validity of an inference, the analyst must attempt to demonstrate that the programme—and not some plausible alternative explanation—is responsible for the effect. In the literature on internal validity, these plausible alternative explanations or factors are often termed "threats" to internal validity.

A number of typical threats to internal validity have been identified. For instance, in a one-group pre-post study a gain from pretest to posttest may be attributable to the programme or to other plausible factors such as historical events occurring between pretest and posttest, or natural maturation over time. Many threats can be ruled out with the inclusion of a control group. Assuming that the control group is equivalent to the programme group prior to the study, the control group pre-post gain will provide evidence for the change which should be attributed to all factors other than the programme.

A different rate of gain in the programme group provides evidence for the relative effect of the programme itself. Thus, we consider randomised experimental designs to be strong in internal validity because of our confidence in the probabilistic pre-programme equivalence between groups which results from random assignment and helps assure that the control group will provide a legitimate reflection of all non-programme factors that might affect outcomes.

In designs that do not use random assignment, the central internal validity concern revolves around the possibility that groups may not be equivalent prior to the programme. We use the term "selection bias" to refer to the case where pre-programme differences between groups are responsible for post-programme differences. Any non-programme factor which is differentially present across groups can constitute a selection bias or a selection threat to internal validity. In RD designs, because of the deliberate pre-programme differences between groups, there are several selection threats to internal validity which might, at first glance, appear to be a problem. For instance, a selection-maturation threat implies that different rates of maturation between groups might explain outcome differences.

For the sake of argument, let's consider a pre-post distribution with a linear relationship having a slope equal to two units. This implies that on the average a person with a given pretest score will have a post-test score two times as high. Clearly there is maturation in this situation, that is, people are getting consistently higher scores over time. If a person has a pretest score of 10 units, we would predict a posttest score of 20 for an absolute gain of 10. But, if a person has a pretest score of 50 we would predict a posttest score of 100 for an absolute gain of 50. Thus the second person naturally gains or matures more in absolute units.

Along these lines, in the RD design we expect that all participants may mature and that in absolute terms this maturation may be different for the two groups on average. Nevertheless, a programme effect in the RD design is not indicated by a difference between the posttest averages of the groups, but rather by a change in the pre-post relationship at the cutoff point. In this example, although we expect different absolute levels of maturation, a single continuous regression line with a slope equal to 2 would describe these different maturational rates.

More to the point, in order for selection-maturation to be a threat to internal validity in RD designs, it must induce a discontinuity in the pre-post relationship which happens to coincide with the cutoff point—an unlikely scenario in most studies. Another selection threat to internal validity which might intuitively seem likely concerns the possibility of differential regression to the mean or a selection-regression threat. The phenomenon of regression to the mean arises when we asymmetrically sample groups from a distribution. On any subsequent measure the obtained sample group mean will be closer to the population mean for that measure than the sample mean from the original distribution is to its population mean.

In RD designs we deliberately create asymmetric samples and consequently expect regression towards the mean in both groups. In general we expect the low-scoring pretest group to evidence a relative gain on the posttest and the high-scoring pretest group to show a relative loss. As with selection-maturation, even though we expect to see differential regression to the mean this poses no problem for the internal validity of the RD design. We don't expect that regression to the mean will result in a discontinuity in the bivariate relationship coincidental with the cutoff point.

In fact, the regression to the mean that will occur is expected to be continuous across the range of the pretest scores and is described by the regression line itself. Although the RD design may initially seem susceptible to selection biases, it is not. The above discussion demonstrates that only factors that would naturally induce a discontinuity in the pre-post relationship could be considered threats to the internal validity of inferences from the RD design.

In principle then the RD design is as strong in internal validity as its randomised experimental alternatives. In practice, however, the validity of the RD design depends directly on how well the analyst can model the true pre-post relationship, certainly a nontrivial statistical problem as is discussed in the statistical analysis of the regression-discontinuity design.

The RD Design and Accountability: It makes sense intuitively that the accountability of a programme is largely dependent on the explicitness of the assignment or allocation of the programme to recipients. Lawmakers and administrators need to recognise that programmes are more evaluable and accountable when the allocation of the programme is more public and verifiable. The three major pre-post designs—the Pre-Post Randomised Experiments, the RD Design, and the Nonequivalent Groups Design—are analogous to the three types of programme allocation schemes which legislators or administrators might choose. Randomised experiments are analogous to the use of a lottery for allocating the programme.

RD designs can be considered explicit, accountable methods for assigning programme recipients on the basis of need or merit. Nonequivalent group designs might be considered a type of political allocation because they enable the use of unverifiable, subjective or politically-motivated assignment. Most social programmes are politically allocated. Even when programmes are allocated primarily on the basis of need or merit, the regulatory agency usually reserves some discretionary capability in deciding who receives the programme.

Without debating the need for such discretion, it is clear that the methodological community should encourage administrators and legislators who wish their programmes to be accountable to make explicit their criteria for programme eligibility by either using probabilistically based lotteries or by relying on quantitative eligibility ratings and cutoff values as in the RD design. To the extent that legislators and administrators can be convinced to move toward more explicit assignment criteria, both the potential utility of the RD design and the accountability of the programmes will be increased.

DESIGNING DESIGNS

Much contemporary social research is devoted to examining whether a programme, treatment, or manipulation causes some outcome or result. For example, we might wish to know whether a new educational programme causes subsequent achievement score gains, whether a special work release programme for prisoners causes lower recidivism rates, whether a novel drug causes a reduction in symptoms, and so on. Cook and Campbell argue that three conditions must be met before we can infer that such a cause-effect relation exists:

— *Covariation*: Changes in the presumed cause must be related to changes in the presumed effect. Thus, if we introduce, remove, or change the level of a treatment or programme, we should observe some change in the outcome measures.

— *Temporal Precedence*: The presumed cause must occur prior to the presumed effect.

— *No Plausible Alternative Explanations*: The presumed cause must be the only reasonable explanation for changes in the outcome measures. If there are other factors which could be responsible for changes in the outcome measures we cannot be confident that the presumed cause-effect relationship is correct.

In most social research the third condition is the most difficult to meet. Any number of factors other than the treatment or programme could cause changes in outcome measures. Campbell and Stanley and later, Cook and Campbell list a number of common plausible alternative explanations. For example, it may be that some historical event which occurs at the same time that the programme or treatment is instituted was responsible for the change in the outcome measures; or, changes in record keeping or measurement systems which occur at the same time as the programme might be falsely attributed to the programme. The reader is referred to standard research methods texts for more detailed discussions of threats to validity.

Minimising Threats to Validity

Good research designs minimise the plausible alternative explanations for the hypothesised cause-effect relationship. But such explanations may be ruled out or minimised in a number of ways other than by design. The discussion which follows outlines five ways to minimise threats to validity, one of which is by research design:

— *By Argument*: The most straightforward way to rule out a potential threat to validity is to simply argue that the threat in question is not a reasonable one. Such an argument may be made either a *priori* or a *posteriori*, although the former will usually be more convincing than the latter. For example, depending on the situation, one might argue that an instrumentation threat is not likely because the same test is used for pre and post test measurements and did not involve observers who might improve, or other such factors. In most cases, ruling out a potential threat to validity by argument alone will be weaker than the other approaches listed below. As a result, the most plausible threats in a study should not, except in unusual cases, be ruled out by argument only.

— *By Measurement or Observation*: In some cases it will be possible to rule out a threat by measuring it and demonstrating that either it does not occur at all or occurs so minimally as to not be a strong alternative explanation for the cause-effect relationship. Consider, for example, a study of the effects of an advertising campaign on subsequent sales of a particular product. In such a study, history would be a plausible alternative explanation. For example, a change in the local economy, the removal of a competing product from the market, or similar events could cause an increase in product sales. One might attempt to minimise such threats by measuring local economic indicators and the availability and sales of competing products. If there is no change in these measures coincident with the onset of the advertising campaign, these threats would be considerably minimised. Similarly, if one is studying the effects of special mathematics training on math achievement scores of children, it might be useful to observe everyday classroom behaviour in order to verify that students were not receiving any additional math training to that provided in the study.

— *By Design*: Here, the major emphasis is on ruling out alternative explanations by adding treatment or control groups, waves of measurement, and the like.

— *By Analysis*: There are a number of ways to rule out alternative explanations using statistical analysis. One interesting example is provided by Jurs and Glass. They suggest that one could study the plausibility of an attrition or mortality threat by conducting a two-way analysis of variance. One factor in this study would be the original treatment group designations, while the other factor would be attrition. The dependent measure could be the pretest or other available pre-programme measures. A main effect on the attrition factor would be indicative of a threat to external validity or generalisability, while an interaction between group and attrition factors would point to a possible threat to internal validity. Where both effects occur, it is reasonable to infer that there is a threat to both internal and external validity.

The plausibility of alternative explanations might also be minimised using covariance analysis. For example, in a study of the effects of "workfare" programmes on social welfare case loads, one plausible alternative explanation might be the status of local economic conditions. Here, it might be possible to construct a measure of economic conditions and include that measure as a covariate in the statistical analysis. One must be careful when using covariance adjustments of this type—"perfect" covariates do not exist in most social research and the use of imperfect covariates will not completely adjust for potential alternative explanations. Nevertheless causal assertions are likely to be strengthened by demonstrating that treatment effects occur even after adjusting on a number of good covariates.

— *By Preventive Action*: When potential threats are anticipated they can often be ruled out by some type of preventive action. For example, if the programme is a desirable one, it is likely that the comparison group would feel jealous or demoralised. Several actions can be taken to minimise the effects of these attitudes including offering the programme to the comparison group upon completion of the study or using programme and comparison groups which have little opportunity for contact and communication. In addition, auditing methods and quality control can be used to track potential experimental dropouts or to insure the standardisation of measurement.

The five categories listed above should not be considered mutually exclusive. The inclusion of measurements designed to minimise threats to validity will obviously be related to the design structure and is likely to be a factor in the analysis. A good research plan should, where possible, make use of multiple methods for reducing threats. In general, reducing a particular threat by design or preventive action will probably be stronger than by using one of the other three approaches. The choice of which strategy to use for any particular threat is complex and depends at least on the cost of the strategy and on the potential seriousness of the threat.

Research Design Construction

Basic Design Elements: Most research designs can be constructed from four basic elements:

- — *Time*: A causal relationship, by its very nature, implies that some time has elapsed between the occurrence of the cause and the consequent effect. While for some phenomena the elapsed time might be measured in microseconds and therefore might be unnoticeable to a casual observer, we normally assume that the cause and effect in social science arenas do not occur simultaneously, In design notation we indicate this temporal element horizontally—whatever symbol is used to indicate the presumed cause would be placed to the left of the symbol indicating measurement of the effect. Thus, as we read from left to right in design notation we are reading across time. Complex designs might involve a lengthy sequence of observations and programmes or treatments across time.
- — *Programme(s) or Treatment(s)*: The presumed cause may be a programme or treatment under the explicit control of the researcher or the occurrence of some natural event or programme not explicitly controlled. In design notation we usually depict a presumed cause with the symbol "X". When multiple programmes or treatments are being studied using the same design, we can keep the programmes distinct by using subscripts such as "X_1" or "X_2". For a comparison group no "X" is used.

— *Observation(s) or Measure(s)*: Measurements are typically depicted in design notation with the symbol "O". If the same measurement or observation is taken at every point in time in a design, then this "O" will be sufficient. Similarly, if the same set of measures is given at every point in time in this study, the "O" can be used to depict the entire set of measures. However, if different measures are given at different times it is useful to subscript the "O" to indicate which measurement is being given at which point in time.

— *Groups or Individuals*: The final design element consists of the intact groups or the individuals who participate in various conditions. Typically, there will be one or more programme and comparison groups. In design notation, each group is indicated on a separate line. Furthermore, the manner in which groups are assigned to the conditions can be indicated by an appropriate symbol at the beginning of each line. Here, "R" will represent a group which was randomly assigned, "N" will depict a group which was nonrandomly assigned and a "C" will indicate that the group was assigned using a cutoff score on a measurement.

Strategy for Design Construction

Considering the basic elements of a research design or the possibilities for expansion are not alone sufficient. We need to be able to integrate these elements with an overall strategy. Furthermore we need to decide which potential threats are best handled by design rather than by argument, measurement, analysis, or preventive action.

While no definitive approach for designing designs exists, we might suggest a tentative strategy based on the notion of expansion discussed above. First, we begin the designing task by setting forth a design which depicts the simple hypothesised causal relationship. Second, we deliberately over-expand this basic design by expanding across time, programme observations, and groups. At this step, the emphasis is on accounting for as many likely alternative explanations as possible using the design. Finally, we then scale back this over-expanded version considering the effect of eliminating each design component. It is at this point that we face the difficult decisions concerning the costs of each design component and the advantages of ruling out specific threats using other approaches.

There are several advantages which result from using this type of approach to design construction. First, we are forced to be explicit about the decisions which are made. Second. the approach is "conservative" in nature. The strategy minimises the chance of our overlooking a major threat to validity in constructing our design. Third, we arrive at a design which is "tailored" to the situation at hand. Finally, the strategy is cost-efficient. Threats which can be accounted for by some other, less costly, approach need not be accounted for in the design itself.

4

Concept Mapping in Research

Concept mapping can be used by research teams to help them clarify and map out the key research issues in an area, to help them operationalise the programmes or interventions or the outcome measures for their study. The concept mapping method isn't the only method around that might help researchers formulate good research problems and projects. Virtually any method that's used to help individuals and groups to think more effectively would probably be useful in research formulation.

Some of the methods that might be included in our toolkit for research formulation might be: brainstorming, brainwriting, nominal group technique, focus groups, Delphi methods, and facet theory. And then, of course, there are all of the methods for identifying relevant literature and previous research work. If you know of any techniques or methods that you think might be useful when formulating the research problem, please feel free to add a notation—if there's a relevant Website, please point to it in the notation.

Probably one of the most common sources of research ideas is the experience of practical problems in the field. Many researchers are directly engaged in social, health or human service programme implementation and come up with their ideas based on what they see happening around them. Others aren't directly involved in service contexts, but work with people who are in order to learn what needs to be better understood. Many of the ideas would strike the outsider as silly or worse.

For instance, in health services areas, there is great interest in the problem of back injuries among nursing staff. It's not necessarily the thing that comes first to mind when we think about the health care field. But if you reflect on it for a minute longer, it should be obvious that nurses and nursing staff do an awful lot of lifting in performing their jobs. They lift and push heavy equipment, and they lift and push often-times heavy patients! If 5 or 10 out of every hundred nursing staff were to strain their backs on average over the period of one year, the costs would be enormous—and that's pretty much what's happening.

Even minor injuries can result in increased absenteeism. Major ones can result in lost jobs and expensive medical bills. The nursing industry figures that this is a problem that costs tens of millions of dollars annually in increased health care. And, the health care industry has developed a number of approaches, many of them educational, to try to reduce the scope and cost of the problem. So, even though it might seem silly at first, many of these practical problems that arise in practice can lead to extensive research efforts. Another source for research ideas is the literature in your specific field. Certainly, many researchers get ideas for research by reading the literature and thinking of ways to extend or refine previous research.

Another type of literature that acts as a source of good research ideas is the Requests For Proposals (RFPs) that are published by government agencies and some companies. These RFPs describe some problem that the agency would like researchers to address—they are virtually handing the researcher an idea! Typically, the RFP describes the problem that needs addressing, the contexts in which it operates, the approach they would like you to take to investigate to address the problem, and the amount they would be willing to pay for such research. Clearly, there's nothing like potential research funding to get researchers to focus on a particular research topic.

And let's not forget the fact that many researchers simply think up their research topic on their own. Of course, no one lives in a vacuum, so we would expect that the ideas you come up with on your own are influenced by your background, culture, education and experiences. Very soon after you get an idea for a study reality begins to kick in and you begin to think about whether the study is feasible at all. There are several major considerations that come into play. Many of these involve making tradeoffs between rigour and practicality. To do a study well from a scientific point of view may force you to do things you wouldn't do normally.

You may have to control the implementation of your programme more carefully than you otherwise might. Or, you may have to ask programme participants lots of questions that you usually wouldn't if you weren't doing research. If you had unlimited resources and unbridled control over the circumstances, you would always be able to do the best quality research. But those ideal circumstances seldom exist, and researchers are almost always forced to look for the best trade-offs they can find in order to get the rigor they desire.

There are several practical considerations that almost always need to be considered when deciding on the feasibility of a research project. First, you have to think about how long the research will take to accomplish. Second, you have to question whether there are important ethical constraints that need consideration. Third, can you achieve the needed cooperation to take the project to its successful conclusion. And fourth, how significant are the costs of conducting the research. Failure to consider any of these factors can mean disaster later.

One of the most important early steps in a research project is the conducting of the literature review. This is also one of the most humbling experiences you're likely to have. Because you're likely to find out that just about any worthwhile idea you will have has been thought of before, at least to some degree. A literature review is designed to identify related research, to set the current research project within a conceptual and theoretical context. When looked at that way, there is almost no topic that is so new or unique that we can't locate relevant and informative related research. Some tips about conducting the literature review. First, concentrate your efforts on the scientific literature.

Try to determine what the most credible research journals are in your topical area and start with those. Put the greatest emphasis on research journals that use a blind review system. In a blind review, authors submit potential articles to a journal editor who solicits several reviewers who agree to give a critical review of the paper. The paper is sent to these reviewers with no identification of the author so that there will be no personal bias. Based on the reviewers' recommendations, the editor can accept the article, reject it, or recommend that the author revise and resubmit it.

Articles in journals with blind review processes can be expected to have a fairly high level of credibility. Second, do the review early in the research process. You are likely to learn a lot in the literature review that will help you in making the trade-offs you'll need to face. After all, previous researchers also had to face tradeoff decisions. First, you might be able to find a study that is quite similar to the one you are thinking of doing. Since all credible research studies have to review the literature themselves, you can check their literature review to get a quick-start on your own.

Second, prior research will help assure that you include all of the major relevant constructs in your study. You may find that other similar studies routinely look at an outcome that you might not have included. If you did your study without that construct, it would not be judged credible if it ignored a major construct. Third, the literature review will help you to find and select appropriate measurement instruments. You will readily see what measurement instruments researchers use themselves in contexts similar to yours. Finally, the literature review will help you to anticipate common problems in your research context. You can use the prior experiences of other to avoid common traps and pitfalls.

CONCEPT MAPPING METHOD

Social scientists have developed a number of methods and processes that might be useful in helping you to formulate a research project. We would include among these at least the following—brainstorming, brainwriting, nominal group techniques, focus groups, affinity mapping, Delphi techniques, facet theory, and qualitative text analysis.

Concept mapping is a general method that can be used to help any individual or group to describe their ideas about some topic in a pictorial form. There are several different types of methods that all currently go by names like "concept mapping", "mental mapping" or "concept webbing." All of them are similar in that they result in a picture of someone's ideas. But the kind of concept mapping we want to describe here is different in a number of important ways.

First, it is primarily a group process and so it is especially well-suited for situations where teams or groups of stakeholders have to work together. The other methods work primarily with individuals. Second, it uses a very structured facilitated approach. There are specific steps that are followed by a trained facilitator in helping a group to articulate its ideas and understand them more clearly. Third, the core of concept mapping consists of several state-of-the-art multivariate statistical methods that analyse the input from all of the individuals and yields an aggregate group product. And fourth, the method requires the use of specialised computer programmes that can handle the data from this type of process and accomplish the correct analysis and mapping procedures.

Although concept mapping is a general method, it is particularly useful for helping social researchers and research teams develop and detail ideas for research. And, it is especially valuable when researchers want to involve relevant stakeholder groups in the act of creating the research project. Although concept mapping is used for many purposes—strategic planning, product development, market analysis, decision- making, measurement development—we concentrate here on it's potential for helping researchers formulate their projects.

Essentially, concept mapping is a structured process, focused on a topic or construct of interest, involving input from one or more participants, that produces an interpretable pictorial view (concept map) of their ideas and concepts and how these are interrelated. Concept mapping helps people to think more effectively as a group without losing their individuality. It helps groups to manage the complexity of their ideas without trivialising them or losing detail. A concept mapping process involves six steps that can take place in a single day or can be spread out over weeks or months depending on the situation.

The first step is the Preparation Step. There are three things done here. The facilitator of the mapping process works with the initiator(s) to identify who the participants will be. A mapping process can have hundreds or even thousands of stakeholders participating, although we usually have a relatively small group of between 10 and 20 stakeholders involved. Second, the initiator works with the stakeholders to develop the focus for the project. For instance, the group might decide to focus on defining a programme or treatment. Or, they might choose to map all of the outcomes they might expect to see as a result. Finally, the group decides on an appropriate schedule for the mapping.

In the Generation Step the stakeholders develop a large set of statements that address the focus. For instance, they might generate statements that describe all of the specific activities that will constitute a specific social programme. Or, they might generate statements describing specific outcomes that might occur as a result of participating in a programme. A wide variety of methods can be used to accomplish this including traditional brainstorming, brainwriting, nominal group techniques, focus groups, qualitative text analysis, and so on. The group can generate up to 200 statements in a concept mapping project.

In the Structuring Step the participants do two things. First, each participant sorts the statements into piles of similar ones. Most times they do this by sorting a deck of cards that has one statement on each card. But they can also do this directly on a computer by dragging the statements into piles that they create. They can have as few or as many piles as they want. Each participant names each pile with a short descriptive label. Second, each participant rates each of the statements on some scale. Usually the statements are rated on a 1-to-5 scale for their relative importance, where a 1 means the statement is relatively unimportant compared to all the rest, a 3 means that it is moderately important, and a 5 means that it is extremely important.

The Representation Step is where the analysis is done—this is the process of taking the sort and rating input and "representing" it in map form. There are two major statistical analyses that are used. The first—multidimensional scaling—takes the sort data across all participants and develops the basic map where each statement is a point on the map and statements that were piled together by more people are closer to each other on the map. The second analysis—cluster analysis—takes the output of the multidimensional scaling and partitions the map into groups of statements or ideas, into clusters. If the statements describe activities of a programme, the clusters show how these can be grouped into logical groups of activities. If the statements are specific outcomes, the clusters might be viewed as outcome constructs or concepts.

In the fifth step—the Interpretation Step—the facilitator works with the stakeholder group to help them develop their own labels and interpretations for the various maps. Finally, the Utilisation Step involves using the maps to help address the original focus. On the programme side, the maps can be used as a visual framework for operationalising the programme. on the outcome side, they can be used as the basis for developing measures and displaying results.

CONCEPT MAPPING PROCESS

The term "structured conceptualisation" refers to any process which can be described as a sequence of concrete operationally-defined steps and which yields a conceptual representation. The specific concept mapping process described here and discussed throughout this volume is considered only one of many possible structured conceptualisation processes. This process can be used whenever there is a group of people who wish to develop a conceptual framework for evaluation or planning, where the framework is displayed in the form of a concept map.

A concept map is a pictorial representation of the group's thinking which displays all of the ideas of the group relative to the topic at hand, shows how these ideas are related to each other and, optionally, shows which ideas are more relevant, important, or appropriate. The scenario within which concept mapping is applied assumes that there is an identifiable group responsible for guiding the evaluation or planning effort.

Depending on the situation, this group might consist of the administrators, staff or members of the board of an organisation; community leaders or representatives of relevant constituency groups; academicians or members of the policy making community; funding agents or representatives of groups with oversight responsibility; representatives of relevant client populations; or combinations of these.

The concept mapping process is guided by a facilitator who could be an outside consultant or an internal member of the group responsible for the planning or evaluation effort. The facilitator's role is only to manage the process—the content, interpretation and utilisation of the concept map are determined entirely by the group. There are six steps in developing a useful group concept map.

Each of these steps will be discussed in some detail and illustrated with data from a concept mapping process which was conducted in York County, Maine, to assist representatives of a number of county human service agencies to develop a conceptual framework for planning services for the elderly. While the major focus of this project was on planning, some comments will be offered regarding the potential use of this conceptualisation for evaluation purposes.

Step 1: Preparation

There are two major tasks which must be undertaken prior to commencement of the actual group process. First, the facilitator must work with the parties involved to decide on who will participate in the process. Second, the facilitator must then work with the participants or a subgroup to decide on the specific focus for the conceptualisation.

Selecting the Participants: One of the most important tasks which the facilitator addresses is who will participate in the concept mapping process. Our experience has been that a conceptualisation is best when it includes a wide variety of relevant people. If we are conducting strategic planning for a human service organisation, we might include administrative staff, service staff, board members, clients, and relevant members of community groups.

In a programme evaluation context, we might similarly include administrators, programme staff, clients, social science theorists, community members, and relevant funding agent representatives. Broad heterogenous participation helps to insure that a wide variety of viewpoints will be considered and encourages a broader range of people to "buy into" the conceptual framework which results. In some situations, however, we have used relatively small homogeneous groups for the conceptualisation process. For instance, if an organisation is beginning a strategic planning effort and would like to lay out quickly some of the major concepts around which the planning will be based, they might prefer to use a relatively small group of administrators and organisational staff members.

The obvious advantage of doing this is that it is logistically simpler to get people together for meetings if they are all on the staff of the organisation. This type of group works well when a quick conceptualisation framework is desired, but in general we would recommend a broader sampling of opinion. In some contexts it might be reasonable to use some random sampling scheme to select participants from a larger defined population. This is most useful when one wishes to argue that the resulting concept map is generalisable to some larger population of interest.

Simple random sampling schemes, of course, run the risk of under representing minority groups from the population and so, if sampling is used, it will typically be best to attempt either some form of stratified random sampling or purposive sampling for heterogeneity. There is no strict limit on the number of people who can be involved in concept mapping. It is feasible, with some process modifications, for an individual to conduct a conceptualisation alone. At the other extreme, we have worked with groups as large as 75-80 people in this process.

Typically, we have had between 10 and 20 people in most of our studies and this seems to be a workable number. Groups of that size insure a variety of opinions and still enable good group discussion and interpretation. It is also not necessary that all participants take part in every step of the process. One might, for instance, have a relatively small group do the generation step, a much larger group perform the structuring and a small group for interpretation and utilisation. In general, however, we have found that concept maps are better understood by people who have participated in all phases of the process than by those who have only taken part in one or two steps.

Developing the Focus: The second major preparatory step involves developing the focus or domain of the conceptualisation. There are two separate products which are desired here. First, the participants must define the focus for the brainstorming session. Second, the focus for ratings which are performed during the structuring step of the process needs to be developed. This essentially involves defining the dimension(s) on which each of the brainstormed statements will be rated. It is essential that the focus for both the brainstorming and the ratings be worded as statements which give the specific instruction intended so that all of the participants can agree in advance.

In developing both the brainstorming and rating focus statements, the facilitator usually has a meeting with the participants or some representative subgroup. In this meeting the facilitator discusses various alternatives for wording each focus and attempts to achieve a group consensus on final choices. For example, the brainstorming focus in a strategic planning process might be worded: "Generate short phrases or sentences which describe specific services which your organisation might provide." Similarly, a rating focus for a programme evaluation might be worded: "Rate each potential outcome on a seven point scale in terms of how strongly you think it will be affected by the programme, where '1' means 'Not at all affected', '4' means 'Moderately affected' and '7' means 'Extremely affected'." The group should agree on the specific wording for each of these focus statements.

The Brainstorming Focus: For any brainstorming session, there are a variety of ways in which the focus can be stated. For instance, if we are interested in strategic planning, participants might focus on the goals of the organisation, the mission of the organisation, or the activities or services which the organisation might provide. Similarly, in programme evaluations they might focus on the nature of the programme, the outcomes they would like to measure, or the types of people they would like to participate in the evaluation.

In defining the brainstorming focus, it is important to try to anticipate the types of statements which will result. For instance, one usually wants to avoid giving double-barrelled focus statements like: "Generate short statements or sentences which describe the goals of our organisation and the needs of our clients" because, when sorting, participants are likely to perceive these two categories as particularly distinct and consequently, they are likely to show up as two major clusters on the final concept map and obscure some of the finer relationships which might be of interest. If both emphases are desired, it would probably be better to conduct two separate conceptualisations to address each issue.

In general, it is best if the final set of brainstormed statements are "of a kind", that is, share the same level of conceptual generality and grammatic structure. For example, a brainstormed set which consists entirely of statements which describe specific services which an organisation might provide and which are all worded in a similar manner would be best if the interest is in conceptualising a taxonomy of potential services.

The Rating Focus: In developing the focus for the ratings, one needs to consider what kind of information will be most useful. In planning, it is often useful to ask the participants to rate how important each brainstormed item is, or how much emphasis should be placed upon it in the planning process. In evaluation, it might be useful to ask them to rate how much effort should be given to various programme components, or how much they believe each outcome is likely to be affected by the programme.

Step 2: Generation of Statements

Once the participants and focus statements have been defined, the actual concept mapping process begins with the generation of a set of statements which ideally should represent the entire conceptual domain for the topic of interest. In the typical case, brainstorming is used and the focus statement constitutes the prompt for the brainstorming session.

The usual rules for brainstorming apply. That is, people are encouraged to generate lots of statements and are told that there should be no criticism or discussion regarding the legitimacy of statements which are generated during the session. Participants are encouraged to ask for clarification of any unfamiliar terms or jargon so that all who participate may understand what was intended by a given statement.

Usually, the facilitator records the statements as they are generated so that all members of the group can see the set of statements as they evolve. We have done this by writing the statements on a blackboard, on sheets of newsprint, or by directly entering them into a computer programme which is displayed on a large screen so that everyone can see the statements. If the facilitator believes that there may be some participants who would be reluctant to state publicly some idea because of its controversial or potentially embarrasing nature, it may be desirable to also allow each participant to submit several statements anonymously on paper so that confidentiality will be preserved.

Theoretically, there is no limit to the number of statements which can be generated. However, large numbers of statements impose serious practical constraints. Based on our experience, we now limit the number of statements to one hundred or less. If the brainstorming session generates more than a hundred statements, we reduce the set. There are a number of ways in which this can be accomplished.

The group as a whole or some subgroup can examine the set of statements for redundancies or ones which can be chosen to represent a set of others. In some instances, we have taken a simple random sample of statements from the larger set and had participants examine the selected set to be sure that no key ideas were being omitted.

For instance, Linton randomly selected 150 statements out of a larger set of 710 statements that were generated. On several occasions we have tried more formal thematic analysis of the text statements using a "key words in context" approach which seems promising. Once a final set of statements has been generated, it is valuable for the group to examine the statements for editing considerations. Sometimes the wording of statements generated in a brainstorming session is awkward or technical jargon is not clear.

In general, each statement should be consistent with what was called for in the brainstorming prompt and should be detailed enough so that every member of the group can understand the essential meaning of the statement. There are many other ways to generate the conceptual domain than brainstorming. Sometimes a set of statements can be abstracted from existing text documents such as annual reports, internal organisational memos, interviews or field notes. For instance, Dumont utilised the "documentary coding method" described by Wrightson to abstract statements or entities from interview records.

In some cases there was no need to generate statements at all because the nature of the conceptualisation dictates the elements of the conceptual domain. Thus, if the goal is to conceptualise the interrelationships between the set of 10 departments in an organisation, we might simply use the 10 department names as the set of statements. Marquart used a set of concepts derived from the literature on employer-sponsored child care as the set of statements for mapping. Caracelli used the 100 items from the California Q-sort as the set of statements.

We have also done some preliminary work to examine the use of outlines for generation where each entry in the outline would be considered a separate statement. One potential advantage of doing this is that we may be able to use the implicit structure of the outline headings and subheadings to structure the conceptual domain directly without asking people to sort the statements. Cooksy describes some preliminary attempts to develop models which take outlines as input and estimate the similarity between statements (based on outline structure) as output.

Step 3: Structuring of Statements

Once we have a set of statements which describes the conceptual domain for a given focus, we minimally need to provide information about how the statements are related to each other. In addition, we often want to rate each statement on some dimension which is defined by the rating focus statement. Both of these tasks constitute the structuring of the conceptual domain. Typically, we obtain information about interrelationships using an unstructured card sorting procedure. Each of the brainstormed statements is printed on a separate 3x5 index card and the complete set of cards is given to each participant.

Each person is then instructed to sort the cards into piles "in a way that makes sense to you." There are several restrictions placed on this procedure: each statement can only be placed in one pile; all statements cannot be put into a single pile; and, all statements cannot be put into their own pile. Except for these conditions, people may pile the cards in any way that makes sense to them. Often the participants perceive that there may be several different ways to sort the cards, all of which make sense. To address this, we have either instructed participants to select the most sensible arrangement or, in some studies, have had each participant sort the cards several times.

Step 4: Representation of Statements

There are three steps involved in the way in which we typically represent the conceptual domain. First, we conduct an analysis which locates each statement as a separate point on a map. Statements which are closer to each other on this map were likely to have been sorted together more frequently; more distant statements on the map were in general sorted together less frequently. Second, we group or partition the statements on this map into clusters which represent higher order conceptual groupings of the original set of statements. Finally, we can construct maps which overlay the averaged ratings either by point or by cluster.

To accomplish the first step, the mapping process, we typically conduct a two-dimensional nonmetric multidimensional scaling of the similarity matrix obtained from Step 3. Nonmetric multidimensional scaling is a technique which takes a proximity matrix and represents it in any number of dimensions as distances between the original items in the matrix. A good introductory discussion of multidimensional scaling can be found in Kruskal and Wish and a more technical description of the algorithm which is used is given in

Davison.

A simple example of the principle which underlies multidimensional scaling can be given. If you were given a geographical map of the United States and asked to construct a table of distances between three major cities, say New York, Chicago, and Los Angeles, you could accomplish this fairly easily. You might take a ruler and measure the distances between each pair of cities and enter them into a 3 x 3 table of ruler-scale relative distances. However, if you were given only a table of distances between the three cities and were asked to draw a map which located the three cities on it as points in a way that fairly represented the relative distances in the table, the task would be slightly more difficult.

You might begin by arbitrarily placing two points on a page to represent two of the cities and then try to draw in a third point so that its distances to the first two cities was proportionate to the distances given in the table. You would be able to accomplish this if the table consisted of three cities, but for more this task would become extremely complex. Multidimensional scaling is a multivariate analysis which accomplishes this task. It takes a table of similarities or distances and iteratively places points on a map so that the original table is as fairly represented as possible.

In concept mapping, the multidimensional scaling analysis creates a map of points which represent the set of statements which were brainstormed based on the similarity matrix which resulted from the sorting task. Typically, when multidimensional scaling analysis conducted the analyst has to specify how many dimensions the set of points is to be fit into. If a one-dimensional solution is requested, all of the points will be arrayed along a single line. A two-dimensional solution places the set of points into a bivariate distribution which is suitable for plotting on an X-Y graph. The analyst could ask for any number of solutions from 1 to N-1 dimensions. However, it is difficult to graph and interpret solutions which are higher than three-dimensional easily.

The literature on multidimensional scaling discusses this dimensionality issue extensively. One view is that the analyst should fit a number of solutions and examine diagnostic statistics to see whether a particular dimensional solution is compelling. This is analogous to examining J-plots of eigenvalues in factor analysis in order to decide on the number of factors. Another view suggests that in certain contexts automatic use of two-dimensional configurations might make sense.

In studies where we have examined other than two-dimensional solutions, we have almost universally found the two-dimensional solution to be acceptable, especially when coupled with cluster analysis as Kruskal and Wish suggest. Therefore, in concept mapping we usually use a two-dimensional multidimensional scaling analysis to map the brainstormed statements into a two-dimensional plot. The second analysis which is conducted to represent the conceptual domain is called hierarchical cluster analysis. This analysis is used to group individual statements on the map into clusters of statements which presumably reflect similar concepts. There are a wide variety of ways to conduct cluster analysis and there is considerable debate in the literature about the relative advantages of different methods.

The discussion centres around ambiguity in the definition of the term "cluster." Everitt and Anderberg present more extensive discussions of this issue. We have tried a number of different cluster analysis approaches. Originally, we used an oblique principle components factor analysis approach to hierarchical cluster analysis where the input for the analysis consisted of the similarity matrix. The problem with this approach was that it often led to results which did not visually correspond with the way in which multidimensional scaling mapped the points. This is because differences in the two algorithms when applied to the same similarity matrix, sometimes meant that points which were close to each other on the map were placed in separate clusters by the cluster analysis.

These results were hard to interpret and seemed to give equal weight to multidimensional scaling and cluster analysis. Instead, it makes sense to view the mathematical basis for multidimensional scaling as stronger than basis for cluster analysis and, accordingly, to rely on the multidimensional scaling rather than cluster analysis to depict the basic inter-statement conceptual similarities. What we wanted was a cluster analysis which grouped or partitioned the statements on the map as they were placed by multidimensional scaling.

We found that this could be accomplished by using the X-Y multidimensional scaling coordinate values for each point as input to the cluster analysis. In addition, we also found that Ward's algorithm for cluster analysis generally gave more sensible and interpretable solutions than other approaches. Therefore we have moved to an approach which uses Ward's hierarchical cluster analysis on the X-Y coordinate data obtained from multidimensional scaling as the standard procedure. This in effect partitions the multidimensional scaling map into any number of clusters.

Just as deciding on the number of dimensions is an essential issue for multidimensional scaling analysis, deciding on the number of clusters is essential for cluster analysis. All hierarchical cluster analysis procedures give as many possible cluster solutions as there are statements. In principle, these clustering methods begin by considering each statement to be its own cluster. At each stage in the analysis, the algorithm combines two clusters until, at the end, all of the statements are in a single cluster.

The task for the analyst is to decide how many clusters the statements should be grouped into for the final solution. There is no simple way to accomplish this task. Essentially, the analyst must use discretion in examining different cluster solutions to decide on which makes sense for the case at hand. Usually, assuming a set of a hundred or fewer statements, we begin by looking at all cluster solutions from about 20 to 3 clusters. Each time the analysis moves from one cluster level to the next lowest we examine which statements were grouped together at that step and attempt to decide whether that grouping makes sense for the statements in the conceptualisation.

In examining different cluster solutions we have found it useful to use a cluster tree which shows pictorially all possible cluster solutions and mergers. In general, we attempt to decide on a cluster solution which, if anything, errs on the side of more clusters than fewer. Clearly this is a task which requires discretion on the part of the analyst and it would be ideal if we could involve the participants directly in this decision-making process, but as of yet we have not determined an easy way to accomplish this kind of task within a group process. Our experience shows that, in general, the cluster analysis results are less interpretable than the results from multidimensional scaling. The cluster analysis is viewed as suggestive and, in some cases, one may want to "visually adjust" the clusters into more sensibly interpretable partitions of the multidimensional space.

The key operative rule here would be to maintain the

integrity of the multidimensional scaling results, that is, try to achieve a clustering solution which does not allow any overlapping clusters. Once we have conducted the multidimensional scaling and cluster analysis, we are able to generate a point and a cluster map. The final analysis involves obtaining average ratings across participants for each statement and for each cluster. These can then be overlayed graphically on the maps to produce the point rating map and the cluster rating map.

We have several products at the end of the representation step. First, we have the two-dimensional point or statement map which locates each of the brainstormed statements as a point. Next to each point we place the number of the statement so that participants can identify each point as a statement. Second, we have a cluster map which shows how the cluster analysis grouped the points. Third, we have the point rating map which shows the average ratings for each statement on the point map. Finally, we also have the cluster rating map which shows the average rating for each cluster on the cluster map. This information forms the basis of the interpretation in the next step.

Step 5: Interpretation of Maps

To interpret the conceptualisation, we usually assemble a specific set of materials and follow a specific sequence of steps—a process which has been worked out largely on the basis of our experiences on many different projects. The materials consist of:

- *The Statement List*: The original list of brainstormed statements, each of which is shown with an identifying number.
- *The Cluster List*: A listing of the statements as they were grouped into clusters by the cluster analysis.

— *The Point Map*: The numbered point map which shows the statements as they were placed by multidimensional scaling.

— *The Cluster Map*: The cluster map which shows how statements were grouped by the cluster analysis.

— *The Point Rating Map*: The numbered point map with average statement ratings overlayed.

— *The Cluster Rating Map*: The cluster map with average cluster ratings overlayed.

Notice that there are four different types of maps here. In fact, they are all concept maps. Each of these maps tells us something about the major ideas and how they are interrelated. Each of them emphasises a different part of the conceptual information. While the maps are distinctly different ways of portraying or representing the conceptual structure, it is important to remember that they are all related to each other and are simply reflecting different sides of the same underlying conceptual phenomenon.

The facilitator begins by giving the group the original set of brainstormed statements and recalling that the statements were generated by them in the brainstorming session. Participants are then reminded that they grouped these statements into piles and told that the individual sortings were combined for the entire group. The statements as they were grouped by the cluster analysis are then presented. Each participant is asked to read through the set of statements for each cluster and come up with a short phrase or word which seems to describe or name the set of statements as a cluster. This is analogous to naming factors in factor analysis.

When each person has a tentative name for each cluster, the group works cluster-by-cluster in an attempt to achieve group agreement on an acceptable name for each cluster. This is an often interesting negotiating task.

When each person in turn gives their name for a certain cluster, the group can often readily see a consensus which exists. For some clusters, the group may have difficulty in arriving at a single name. This is because the statements in that cluster might actually contain several different ideas and, had a higher cluster solution been selected, the statements would have been subdivided into subclusters. In these cases, the facilitator might suggest that the group use a hybrid name, perhaps by combining titles from several individuals. In any event, the group is told that these names are tentative and may be revised later.

Step 6: Utilisation of Maps

At this point in the process we turn our attention back to the original reason for conducting the structured conceptualisation. The group discusses how the final concept map might be used to enhance either the planning or evaluation effort. The uses of the map are limited only by the creativity and motivation of the group. A number of straightforward applications suggest themselves. For instance, if the conceptualisation was done as the basis for planning, the final map might be used for structuring the subsequent planning effort. The planning group might use it for dividing up into subgroups or task forces, each of which is assigned a specific cluster or region.

Each task group could then examine issues like: the organisational budget allocation for each cluster, how organisational personnel are distributed within each cluster, how important each cluster is relative to the others, what resources might be brought to bear in addressing each cluster, what level of competition exists from other organisations providing services in each cluster, and so on. The task forces can use the individual statements within a cluster as cues or prompts concerning what they should consider specifically within each cluster.

For planning purposes, the concept map can also be used as the framework for an outline of a planning report. Regional headings would constitute the highest level of indentation for the outline, clusters would be subheaded within their appropriate regions, individual statements could be subheadings within clusters, and any statement-level information relevant to planning could be subheaded within this structure. Thus for planning, the concept map provides a framework for understanding important issues in a way which enables sensible pictorial and outline representations.

The concept map is also extremely useful in evaluation contexts. Here, its utilisation depends on what the focus was for the conceptualisation. If the focus was on planning a programme or service which would then be evaluated, the concept map can act as an organising device for operationalising and implementing the programme. For instance, if the programme is a training programme in a human service agency, the training can be constructed based on the concept map with different training sessions designed to address each cluster and the individual brainstormed statements acting as cues for what kinds of information should be covered in each session.

The concept map is the framework for the programme construct and can form the basis of a process evaluation of the programme. In this case or in the case where the focus of the conceptualisation was on the outcomes of some programme, the concept map can guide measurement development. Each cluster can be viewed as a measurement construct and the individual statements can suggest specific operationalisations of measures within constructs. For instance, if the group wished to develop a questionnaire, they could use the concept map by having each cluster represented with questions on the questionnaire.

Furthermore, the original brainstormed statements might provide question prompts which either directly or with some revision could be included on the questionnaire along with some rating response format. Alternatively, if a more multimethod approach to measurement was desired, the group could make sure that within each cluster several different types of measures were constructed to reflect the cluster. The exciting prospect here is that the concept map provides a useful way to operationalise the multitrait-multimethod approach to measurement which was outlined by Campbell and Fiske and is described in greater detail in the paper by Davis.

In this example, the concept map represents the group's theoretical expectations about how the major measurement constructs are conceptually interrelated. From the concept map we can predict the rank order which we expect in the correlations between measures. These expectations could then be directly compared with a matrix of correlations as obtained in the study and the degree to which the two match can constitute evidence for the construct validity of the measures. This "pattern matching" approach to construct validity is discussed in detail in Trochim.

Valentine used concept mapping to construct an instrument which could be used to assess caring in a nursing context.

5

Sampling

Sampling is the process of selecting units from a population of interest so that by studying the sample we may fairly generalise our results back to the population from which they were chosen. Let's begin by covering some of the key terms in sampling like "population" and "sampling frame." Then, because some types of sampling rely upon quantitative models, we'll talk about some of the statistical terms used in sampling.

EXTERNAL VALIDITY

External validity is related to generalising. That's the major thing you need to keep in mind. Recall that validity refers to the approximate truth of propositions, inferences, or conclusions. So, external validity refers to the approximate truth of conclusions the involve generalisations. Put in more pedestrian terms, external validity is the degree to which the conclusions in your study would hold for other persons in other places and at other times.

In science there are two major approaches to how we provide evidence for a generalisation. The first approach is the Sampling Model. In the sampling model, you start by identifying the population you would like to generalise to. Then, you draw a fair sample from that population and conduct your research with the sample. Finally, because the sample is representative of the population, you can automatically generalise your results back to the population. There are several problems with this approach.

First, perhaps you don't know at the time of your study who you might ultimately like to generalise to. Second, you may not be easily able to draw a fair or representative sample. Third, it's impossible to sample across all times that you might like to generalise to (like next year). A threat to external validity is an explanation of how you might be wrong in making a generalisation. For instance, you conclude that the results of your study can be generalised to another context. There are three major threats to external validity because there are three ways you could be wrong—people, places or times.

Your critics could come along, for example, and argue that the results of your study are due to the unusual type of people who were in the study. Or, they could argue that it might only work because of the unusual place you did the study in. Or, they might suggest that you did your study in a peculiar time. For instance, if you did your smoking cessation study the week after the Surgeon General issues the well-publicised results of the latest smoking and cancer studies, you might get different results than if you had done it the week before.

One way, based on the sampling model, suggests that you do a good job of drawing a sample from a population. For instance, you should use random selection, if possible, rather than a nonrandom procedure. And, once selected, you should try to assure that the respondents participate in your study and that you keep your dropout rates low. A second approach would be to use the theory of proximal similarity more effectively. Perhaps you could do a better job of describing the ways your contexts and others differ, providing lots of data about the degree of similarity between various groups of people, places, and even times.

You might even be able to map out the degree of proximal similarity among various contexts with a methodology like concept mapping. Perhaps the best approach to criticisms of generalisations is simply to show them that they're wrong—do your study in a variety of places, with different people and at different times. That is, your external validity will be stronger the more you replicate your study.

CONCEPTS OF SAMPLING PROCESS

As with anything else in life you have to learn the language of an area if you're going to ever hope to use it. Here, we want to introduce several different terms for the major groups that are involved in a sampling process and the role that each group plays in the logic of sampling. The major question that motivates sampling in the first place is: "Who do you want to generalise to?" Or should it be: "To whom do you want to generalise?" In most social research we are interested in more than just the people who directly participate in our study. We would like to be able to talk in general terms and not be confined only to the people who are in our study.

Now, there are times when we aren't very concerned about generalising. Maybe we're just evaluating a programme in a local agency and we don't care whether the programme would work with other people in other places and at other times. In that case, sampling and generalising might not be of interest. In other cases, we would really like to be able to generalise almost universally. When psychologists do research, they are often interested in developing theories that would hold for all humans. But in most applied social research, we are interested in generalising to specific groups.

The group you wish to generalise to is often called the population in your study. This is the group you would like to sample from because this is the group you are interested in generalising to. Let's imagine that you wish to generalise to urban homeless males between the ages of 30 and 50 in India. If that is the population of interest, you are likely to have a very hard time developing a reasonable sampling plan. You are probably not going to find an accurate listing of this population, and even if you did, you would almost certainly not be able to mount a national sample across hundreds of urban areas.

So we probably should make a distinction between the population you would like to generalise to, and the population that will be accessible to you. We'll call the former the theoretical population and the latter the accessible population. Once you've identified the theoretical and accessible populations, you have to do one more thing before you can actually draw a sample—you have to get a list of the members of the accessible population.

The listing of the accessible population from which you'll draw your sample is called the sampling frame. If you were doing a phone survey and selecting names from the telephone directory, the book would be your sampling frame. That wouldn't be a great way to sample because significant subportions of the population either don't have a phone or have moved in or out of the area since the last directory was printed. Notice that in this case, you might identify the area code and all three-digit prefixes within that area code and draw a sample simply by randomly dialing numbers or random-digit-dialing.

In this case, the sampling frame is not a list per se, but is rather a procedure that you follow as the actual basis for sampling. Finally, you actually draw your sample. The sample is the group of people who you select to be in your study. You may not be able to contact or recruit all of the people you actually sample, or some could drop out over the course of the study. The group that actually completes your study is a subsample of the sample—it doesn't include nonrespondents or dropouts.

SAMPLING DISTRIBUTION

A crucial midway concept you need to understand is the sampling distribution. In order to understand it, you have to be able and willing to do a thought experiment. Imagine that instead of just taking a single sample like we do in a typical study, you took three independent samples of the same population. And furthermore, imagine that for each of your three samples, you collected a single response and computed a single statistic, say, the mean of the response. Even though all three samples came from the same population, you wouldn't expect to get the exact same statistic from each.

They would differ slightly just due to the random "luck of the draw" or to the natural fluctuations or vagaries of drawing a sample. But you would expect that all three samples would yield a similar statistical estimate because they were drawn from the same population. Now, for the leap of imagination! Imagine that you did an infinite number of samples from the same population and computed the average for each one. If you plotted them on a histogram or bar graph you should find that most of them converge on the same central value and that you get fewer and fewer samples that have averages farther away up or down from that central value.

In other words, the bar graph would be well described by the bell curve shape that is an indication of a "normal" distribution in statistics. The distribution of an infinite number of samples of the same size as the sample in your study is known as the sampling distribution. When we keep the sampling distribution in mind, we realise that while the statistic we got from our sample is probably near the center of the sampling distribution we could have gotten one of the extreme samples just by the luck of the draw.

If we take the average of the sampling distribution—the average of the averages of an infinite number of samples—we would be much closer to the true population average—the parameter of interest. So the average of the sampling distribution is essentially equivalent to the parameter. But the standard deviation of the sampling distribution tells us something about how different samples would be distributed.

SAMPLING ERROR

In sampling contexts, the standard error is called sampling error. Sampling error gives us some idea of the precision of our statistical estimate. A low sampling error means that we had relatively less variability or range in the sampling distribution. But here we go again—we never actually see the sampling distribution! So how do we calculate sampling error? We base our calculation on the standard deviation of our sample.

The greater the sample standard deviation, the greater the standard error. The standard error is also related to the sample size. The greater your sample size, the smaller the standard error. Because the greater the sample size, the closer your sample is to the actual population itself. If you take a sample that consists of the entire population you actually have no sampling error because you don't have a sample, you have the entire population. In that case, the mean you estimate is the parameter.

PROBABILITY SAMPLING METHOD

A probability sampling method is any method of sampling that utilises some form of random selection. In order to have a random selection method, you must set up some process or procedure that assures that the different units in your population have equal probabilities of being chosen. Humans have long practiced various forms of random selection, such as picking a name out of a hat, or choosing the short straw. These days, we tend to use computers as the mechanism for generating random numbers as the basis for random selection.

Some Basic Terms

Before we can explain the various probability methods we have to define some basic terms. These are:

- N = the number of cases in the sampling frame
- n = the number of cases in the sample
- NCn = the number of combinations (subsets) of n from N
- f = n/N = the sampling fraction

That's it. With those terms defined we can begin to define the different probability sampling methods.

Simple Random Sampling

The simplest form of random sampling is called simple random sampling. Pretty tricky, huh? Here's the quick description of simple random sampling:

- *Objective*: To select n units out of N such that each NCn has an equal chance of being selected.
- *Procedure*: Use a table of random numbers, a computer random number generator, or a mechanical device to select the sample.

A somewhat stilted, if accurate, definition. Let's see if we can make it a little more real.

Let's assume that we are doing some research with a small service agency that wishes to assess client's views of quality of service over the past year. First, we have to get the sampling frame organised. To accomplish this, we'll go through agency records to identify every client over the past 12 months. If we're lucky, the agency has good accurate computerised records and can quickly produce such a list. Then, we have to actually draw the sample. Decide on the number of clients you would like to have in the final sample. For the sake of the example, let's say you want to select 100 clients to survey and that there were 1000 clients over the past 12 months.

Then, the sampling fraction is f = n/N = 100/1000 =.10 or 10%. Now, to actually draw the sample, you have several options. You could print off the list of 1000 clients, tear then into separate strips, put the strips in a hat, mix them up real good, close your eyes and pull out the first 100. But this mechanical procedure would be tedious and the quality of the sample would depend on how thoroughly you mixed them up and how randomly you reached in. Perhaps a better procedure would be to use the kind of ball machine that is popular with many of the state lotteries. You would need three sets of balls numbered 0 to 9, one set for each of the digits from 000 to 999.

Number the list of names from 1 to 1000 and then use the ball machine to select the three digits that selects each person. The obvious disadvantage here is that you need to get the ball machines. Neither of these mechanical procedures is very feasible and, with the development of inexpensive computers there is a much easier way. Here's a simple procedure that's especially useful if you have the names of the clients already on the computer. Many computer programmes can generate a series of random numbers. Let's assume you can copy and paste the list of client names into a column in an EXCEL spreadsheet. Then, in the column right next to it paste the function =RAND which is EXCEL's way of putting a random number between 0 and 1 in the cells. Then, sort both columns—the list of names and the random number—by the random numbers. This rearranges the list in random order from the lowest to the highest random number. Then, all you have to do is take the first hundred names in this sorted list. pretty simple. You could probably accomplish the whole thing in under a minute.

Simple random sampling is simple to accomplish and is easy to explain to others. Because simple random sampling is a fair way to select a sample, it is reasonable to generalise the results from the sample back to the population. Simple random sampling is not the most statistically efficient method of sampling and you may, just because of the luck of the draw, not get good representation of subgroups in a population. To deal with these issues, we have to turn to other sampling methods.

Stratified Random Sampling

Stratified Random Sampling, also sometimes called proportional or quota random sampling, involves dividing your population into homogeneous subgroups and then taking a simple random sample in each subgroup. In more formal terms:

> Objective: Divide the population into non-overlapping groups N1, N2, N3,... Ni, such that N1 + N2 + N3 +... + Ni = N. Then do a simple random sample of f = n/N in each strata.

There are several major reasons why you might prefer stratified sampling over simple random sampling. First, it assures that you will be able to represent not only the overall population, but also key subgroups of the population, especially small minority groups. If you want to be able to talk about subgroups, this may be the only way to effectively assure you'll be able to. If the subgroup is extremely small, you can use different sampling fractions (f) within the different strata to randomly over-sample the small group.

When we use the same sampling fraction within strata we are conducting proportionate stratified random sampling. When we use different sampling fractions in the strata, we call this disproportionate stratified random sampling. Second, stratified random sampling will generally have more statistical precision than simple random sampling. This will only be true if the strata or groups are homogeneous. If they are, we expect that the variability within-groups is lower than the variability for the population as a whole. Stratified sampling capitalises on that fact. For example, let's say that the population of clients for our agency can be divided into three groups: Caucasian, African-American and Hispanic-American. Furthermore, let's assume that both the African-Americans and Hispanic-Americans are relatively small minorities of the clientele.

If we just did a simple random sample of n=100 with a sampling fraction of 10%, we would expect by chance alone that we would only get 10 and 5 persons from each of our two smaller groups. And, by chance, we could get fewer than that! If we stratify, we can do better. First, let's determine how many people we want to have in each group. Let's say we still want to take a sample of 100 from the population of 1000 clients over the past year. But we think that in order to say anything about subgroups we will need at least 25 cases in each group. So, let's sample 50 Caucasians, 25 African-Americans, and 25 Hispanic-Americans.

We know that 10% of the population, or 100 clients, are African-American. If we randomly sample 25 of these, we have a within-stratum sampling fraction of 25/100 = 25%. Similarly, we know that 5% or 50 clients are Hispanic-American. So our within-stratum sampling fraction will be 25/50 = 50%. Finally, by subtraction we know that there are 850 Caucasian clients. Our within-stratum sampling fraction for them is 50/850 = about 5.88%. Because the groups are more homogeneous within-group than across the population as a whole, we can expect greater statistical precision. And, because we stratified, we know we will have enough cases from each group to make meaningful subgroup inferences.

Systematic Random Sampling

Here are the steps you need to follow in order to achieve a systematic random sample:

— number the units in the population from 1 to N

— decide on the n (sample size) that you want or need

— k = N/n = the interval size

— randomly select an integer between 1 to k

— then take every k^{th} unit

All of this will be much clearer with an example. Let's assume that we have a population that only has N=100 people in it and that you want to take a sample of n=20. To use systematic sampling, the population must be listed in a random order. The sampling fraction would be f = 20/100 = 20%. In this case, the interval size, k, is equal to N/n = 100/20 = 5. Now, select a random integer from 1 to 5. In our example, imagine that you chose 4. Now, to select the sample, start with the 4th unit in the list and take every k^{th} unit (every 5th, because k=5). You would be sampling units 4, 9, 14, 19, and so on to 100 and you would wind up with 20 units in your sample.

For this to work, it is essential that the units in the population are randomly ordered, at least with respect to the characteristics you are measuring. For one thing, it is fairly easy to do. You only have to select a single random number to start things off. It may also be more precise than simple random sampling. Finally, in some situations there is simply no easier way to do random sampling.

Cluster Sampling Methods

The problem with random sampling methods when we have to sample a population that's disbursed across a wide geographic region is that you will have to cover a lot of ground geographically in order to get to each of the units you sampled. Imagine taking a simple random sample of all the residents of N.C.R. New Delhi in order to conduct personal interviews. By the luck of the draw you will wind up with respondents who come from all over the state. Your interviewers are going to have a lot of travelling to do. It is for precisely this problem that cluster or area random sampling was invented.

In cluster sampling, we follow these steps:

— divide population into clusters (usually along geographic boundaries)

— randomly sample clusters

— measure all units within sampled clusters.

Multi-Stage Sampling

The four methods we've covered so far—simple, stratified, systematic and cluster—are the simplest random sampling strategies. In most real applied social research, we would use sampling methods that are considerably more complex than these simple variations.

The most important principle here is that we can combine the simple methods described earlier in a variety of useful ways that help us address our sampling needs in the most efficient and effective manner possible. When we combine sampling methods, we call this multi-stage sampling. For example, consider the idea of sampling N.C.R New Delhi residents for face-to-face interviews. Clearly we would want to do some type of cluster sampling as the first stage of the process. We might sample townships or census tracts throughout the state. But in cluster sampling we would then go on to measure everyone in the clusters we select.

Even if we are sampling census tracts we may not be able to measure everyone who is in the census tract. So, we might set up a stratified sampling process within the clusters. In this case, we would have a two-stage sampling process with stratified samples within cluster samples. Or, consider the problem of sampling students in grade schools. We might begin with a national sample of school districts stratified by economics and educational level. Within selected districts, we might do a simple random sample of schools.

Within schools, we might do a simple random sample of classes or grades. And, within classes, we might even do a simple random sample of students. In this case, we have three or four stages in the sampling process and we use both stratified and simple random sampling. By combining different sampling methods we are able to achieve a rich variety of probabilistic sampling methods that can be used in a wide range of social research contexts.

NONPROBABILITY AND PROBABILITY SAMPLING

The difference between nonprobability and probability sampling is that nonprobability sampling does not involve random selection and probability sampling does. Does that mean that nonprobability samples aren't representative of the population? Not necessarily. But it does mean that nonprobability samples cannot depend upon the rationale of probability theory. At least with a probabilistic sample, we know the odds or probability that we have represented the population well. We are able to estimate confidence intervals for the statistic. With nonprobability samples, we may or may not represent the population well, and it will often be hard for us to know how well we've done so.

In general, researchers prefer probabilistic or random sampling methods over nonprobabilistic ones, and consider them to be more accurate and rigorous. However, in applied social research there may be circumstances where it is not feasible, practical or theoretically sensible to do random sampling. Here, we consider a wide range of nonprobabilistic alternatives. We can divide nonprobability sampling methods into two broad types: accidental or purposive. Most sampling methods are purposive in nature because we usually approach the sampling problem with a specific plan in mind. The most important distinctions among these types of sampling methods are the ones between the different types of purposive sampling approaches.

Convenience Sampling

One of the most common methods of sampling goes under the various titles listed here. We would include in this category the traditional "man on the street" interviews conducted frequently by television news programmes to get a quick reading of public opinion. We would also argue that the typical use of college students in much psychological research is primarily a matter of convenience. In clinical practice, we might use clients who are available to us as our sample. In many research contexts, we sample simply by asking for volunteers. Clearly, the problem with all of these types of samples is that we have no evidence that they are representative of the populations we're interested in generalising to—and in many cases we would clearly suspect that they are not.

Purposive Sampling

In purposive sampling, we sample with a purpose in mind. We usually would have one or more specific predefined groups we are seeking. For instance, have you ever run into people in a mall or on the street who are carrying a clipboard and who are stopping various people and asking if they could interview them? Most likely they are conducting a purposive sample. They might be looking for South Indian females between 30-40 years old. They size up the people passing by and anyone who looks to be in that category they stop to ask if they will participate.

One of the first things they're likely to do is verify that the respondent does in fact meet the criteria for being in the sample. Purposive sampling can be very useful for situations where you need to reach a targeted sample quickly and where sampling for proportionality is not the primary concern. With a purposive sample, you are likely to get the opinions of your target population, but you are also likely to overweight subgroups in your population that are more readily accessible.

All of the methods that follow can be considered subcategories of purposive sampling methods. We might sample for specific groups or types of people as in modal instance, expert, or quota sampling. We might sample for diversity as in heterogeneity sampling. Or, we might capitalise on informal social networks to identify specific respondents who are hard to locate otherwise, as in snowball sampling. In all of these methods we know what we want—we are sampling with a purpose.

Modal Instance Sampling

In statistics, the mode is the most frequently occurring value in a distribution. In sampling, when we do a modal instance sample, we are sampling the most frequent case, or the "typical" case. In a lot of informal public opinion polls, for instance, they interview a "typical" voter. There are a number of problems with this sampling approach. First, how do we know what the "typical" or "modal" case is? We could say that the modal voter is a person who is of average age, educational level, and income in the population. But, it's not clear that using the averages of these is the fairest. And, how do you know that those three variables—age, education, income—are the only or event the most relevant for classifying the typical voter? What if religion or ethnicity is an important discriminator? Clearly, modal instance sampling is only sensible for informal sampling contexts.

Expert Sampling

Expert sampling involves the assembling of a sample of persons with known or demonstrable experience and expertise in some area. Often, we convene such a sample under the auspices of a "panel of experts." There are actually two reasons you might do expert sampling. First, because it would be the best way to elicit the views of persons who have specific expertise. In this case, expert sampling is essentially just a specific subcase of purposive sampling. But the other reason you might use expert sampling is to provide evidence for the validity of another sampling approach you've chosen.

For instance, let's say you do modal instance sampling and are concerned that the criteria you used for defining the modal instance are subject to criticism. You might convene an expert panel consisting of persons with acknowledged experience and insight into that field or topic and ask them to examine your modal definitions and comment on their appropriateness and validity. The advantage of doing this is that you aren't out on your own trying to defend your decisions—you have some acknowledged experts to back you. The disadvantage is that even the experts can be, and often are, wrong.

Quota Sampling

In quota sampling, you select people nonrandomly according to some fixed quota. There are two types of quota sampling: proportional and non proportional. In proportional quota sampling you want to represent the major characteristics of the population by sampling a proportional amount of each. For instance, if you know the population has 40% women and 60% men, and that you want a total sample size of 100, you will continue sampling until you get those percentages and then you will stop.

So, if you've already got the 40 women for your sample, but not the sixty men, you will continue to sample men but even if legitimate women respondents come along, you will not sample them because you have already "met your quota." The problem here is that you have to decide the specific characteristics on which you will base the quota. Nonproportional quota sampling is a bit less restrictive. In this method, you specify the minimum number of sampled units you want in each category. here, you're not concerned with having numbers that match the proportions in the population. Instead, you simply want to have enough to assure that you will be able to talk about even small groups in the population. This method is the nonprobabilistic analogue of stratified random sampling in that it is typically used to assure that smaller groups are adequately represented in your sample.

Heterogeneity Sampling

We sample for heterogeneity when we want to include all opinions or views, and we aren't concerned about representing these views proportionately. Another term for this is sampling for diversity. In many brainstorming or nominal group processes, we would use some form of heterogeneity sampling because our primary interest is in getting broad spectrum of ideas, not identifying the "average" or "modal instance" ones.

In effect, what we would like to be sampling is not people, but ideas. We imagine that there is a universe of all possible ideas relevant to some topic and that we want to sample this population, not the population of people who have the ideas. Clearly, in order to get all of the ideas, and especially the "outlier" or unusual ones, we have to include a broad and diverse range of participants. Heterogeneity sampling is, in this sense, almost the opposite of modal instance sampling.

Snowball Sampling

In snowball sampling, you begin by identifying someone who meets the criteria for inclusion in your study. You then ask them to recommend others who they may know who also meet the criteria. Although this method would hardly lead to representative samples, there are times when it may be the best method available.

Snowball sampling is especially useful when you are trying to reach populations that are inaccessible or hard to find. For instance, if you are studying the homeless, you are not likely to be able to find good lists of homeless people within a specific geographical area. However, if you go to that area and identify one or two, you may find that they know very well who the other

6

Measurement

Measurement is the process observing and recording the observations that are collected as part of a research effort. There are two major issues that will be considered here. First, you have to understand the fundamental ideas involved in measuring. Here we consider two of major measurement concepts.

Second, you have to understand the different types of measures that you might use in social research. We consider four broad categories of measurements. Survey research includes the design and implementation of interviews and questionnaires. Scaling involves consideration of the major methods of developing and implementing a scale. Qualitative research provides an overview of the broad range of non-numerical measurement approaches. And unobtrusive measures presents a variety of measurement methods that don't intrude on or interfere with the context of the research.

VALIDITY OF MEASURES

There's an awful lot of confusion in the methodological literature that stems from the wide variety of labels that are used to describe the validity of measures. We want to make two cases here. First, it's dumb to limit our scope only to the validity of measures. We really want to talk about the validity of any operationalisation. That is, any time you translate a concept or construct into a functioning and operating reality, you need to be concerned about how well you did the translation. This issue is as relevant when we are talking about treatments or programmes as it is when we are talking about measures. Second, we want to use the term construct validity to refer to the general case of translating any construct into an operationalisation. Let's use all of the other validity terms to reflect different ways you can demonstrate different aspects of construct validity.

With all that in mind, here's a list of the validity types that are typically mentioned in texts and research papers when talking about the quality of measurement:

— Construct validity.

— Translation validity.

— Face validity.

— Content validity.

— Criterion-related validity.

— Predictive validity.

— Concurrent validity.

— Convergent validity.

— Discriminant validity.

Construct Validity

Construct validity refers to the degree to which inferences can legitimately be made from the operationalisations in your study to the theoretical constructs on which those operationalisations were based. Construct validity is related to generalising. But, where external validity involves generalising from your study context to other people, places or times, construct validity involves generalising from your programme or measures to the concept of your programme or measures.

When we claim that our programmes or measures have construct validity, we are essentially claiming that we as researchers understand how our constructs or theories of the programmes and measures operate in theory and we claim that we can provide evidence that they behave in practice the way we think they should. The researcher essentially has a theory of how the programmes and measures related to each other, a theoretical pattern if you will. And, the researcher provides evidence through observation that the programmes or measures actually behave that way in reality, an observed pattern.

When we claim construct validity, we're essentially claiming that our observed pattern—how things operate in reality—corresponds with our theoretical pattern—how we think the world works. Construct validity refers to the degree to which inferences can legitimately be made from the operationalisations in your study to the theoretical constructs on which those operationalisations were based.

Construct validity is an assessment of how well you translated your ideas or theories into actual programmes or measures. Because when you think about the world or talk about it with others you are using words that represent concepts. If you tell someone that a special type of math tutoring will help their child do better in math, you are communicating at the level of concepts or constructs. You aren't describing in operational detail the specific things that the tutor will do with their child. You aren't describing the specific questions that will be on the math test that their child will do better on.

You are talking in general terms, using constructs. If you based your recommendation on research that showed that the special type of tutoring improved children' math scores, you would want to be sure that the type of tutoring you are referring to is the same as what that study implemented and that the type of outcome you're saying should occur was the type they measured in their study. Otherwise, you would be mislabelling or misrepresenting the research. In this sense, construct validity can be viewed as a "truth in labelling" kind of issue.

Translation Validity

Both of those face and content validity types are attempting to assess the degree to which you accurately translated your construct into the operationalisation, and hence the choice of name. Let's look at the two types of translation validity.

Face Validity

In face validity, you look at the operationalisation and see whether "on its face" it seems like a good translation of the construct. This is probably the weakest way to try to demonstrate construct validity. For instance, you might look at a measure of math ability, read through the questions, and decide that yep, it seems like this is a good measure of math ability. Or, you might observe a teenage pregnancy prevention programme and conclude that, "Yep, this is indeed a teenage pregnancy prevention programme."

Of course, if this is all you do to assess face validity, it would clearly be weak evidence because it is essentially a subjective judgement call. We can improve the quality of face validity assessment considerably by making it more systematic. For instance, if you are trying to assess the face validity of a math ability measure, it would be more convincing if you sent the test to a carefully selected sample of experts on math ability testing and they all reported back with the judgement that your measure appears to be a good measure of math ability.

Content Validity

In content validity, you essentially check the operationalisation against the relevant content domain for the construct. This approach assumes that you have a good detailed description of the content domain, something that's not always true. For instance, we might lay out all of the criteria that should be met in a programme that claims to be a "teenage pregnancy prevention programme." We would probably include in this domain specification the definition of the target group, criteria for deciding whether the programme is preventive in nature, and lots of criteria that spell out the content that should be included like basic information on pregnancy, the use of abstinence, birth control methods, and so on.

Then, armed with these criteria, we could use them as a type of checklist when examining our programme. Only programmes that meet the criteria can legitimately be defined as "teenage pregnancy prevention programmes." This all sounds fairly straightforward, and for many operationalisations it will be. But for other constructs, it will not be easy to decide on the criteria that constitute the content domain.

Criteria-Related Validity

In criteria-related validity, you check the performance of your operationalisation against some criterion. In content validity, the criteria are the construct definition itself—it is a direct comparison. In criterion-related validity, we usually make a prediction about how the operationalisation will perform based on our theory of the construct. The differences among the different criterion-related validity types is in the criteria they use as the standard for judgement.

Predictive Validity

In predictive validity, we assess the operationalisation's ability to predict something it should theoretically be able to predict. For instance, we might theorise that a measure of math ability should be able to predict how well a person will do in an engineering-based profession. We could give our measure to experienced engineers and see if there is a high correlation between scores on the measure and their salaries as engineers. A high correlation would provide evidence for predictive validity—it would show that our measure can correctly predict something that we theoretically think it should be able to predict.

Concurrent Validity

In concurrent validity, we assess the operationalisation's ability to distinguish between groups that it should theoretically be able to distinguish between. For example, if we come up with a way of assessing manic-depression, our measure should be able to distinguish between people who are diagnosed manic-depression and those diagnosed paranoid schizophrenic. If we want to assess the concurrent validity of a new measure of empowerment, we might give the measure to both migrant farm workers and to the farm owners, theorising that our measure should show that the farm owners are higher in empowerment. As in any discriminating test, the results are more powerful if you are able to show that you can discriminate between two groups that are very similar.

Convergent Validity

In convergent validity, we examine the degree to which the operationalisation is similar to other operationalisations that it theoretically should be similar to. For instance, to show the convergent validity of a Head Start programme, we might gather evidence that shows that the programme is similar to other Head Start programmes. Or, to show the convergent validity of a test of arithmetic skills, we might correlate the scores on our test with scores on other tests that purport to measure basic math ability, where high correlations would be evidence of convergent validity.

Discriminant Validity

In discriminant validity, we examine the degree to which the operationalisation is not similar to (diverges from) other operationalisations that it theoretically should not be similar to. For instance, to show the discriminant validity of a Head Start programme, we might gather evidence that shows that the programme is not similar to other early childhood programmes that don't label themselves as Head Start programmes. Or, to show the discriminant validity of a test of arithmetic skills, we might correlate the scores on our test with scores on tests that of verbal ability, where low correlations would be evidence of discriminant validity. To establish discriminant validity, you need to show that measures that should not be related are in reality not related.

RELIABILITY

Reliability has to do with the quality of measurement. In its everyday sense, reliability is the "consistency" or "repeatability" of your measures. Before we can define reliability precisely we have to lay the groundwork. First, you have to learn about the foundation of reliability, the true score theory of measurement. Along with that, you need to understand the different types of measurement error because errors in measures play a key role in degrading reliability.

With this foundation, you can consider the basic theory of reliability, including a precise definition of reliability. There you will find out that we cannot calculate reliability—we can only estimate it. Because of this, there a variety of different types of reliability that each have multiple ways to estimate reliability for that type. In the end, it's important to integrate the idea of reliability with the other major criteria for the quality of measurement—validity—and develop an understanding of the relationships between reliability and validity in measurement.

True Score Theory

True Score Theory is a theory about measurement. Like all theories, you need to recognise that it is not proven—it is postulated as a model of how the world operates. Like many very powerful model, the true score theory is a very simple one. Essentially, true score theory maintains that every measurement is an additive composite of two components: true ability of the respondent on that measure; and random error.

We observe the measurement—the score on the test, the total for a self-esteem instrument, the scale value for a person's weight. We don't observe what's on the right side of the equation, we assume that there are two components to the right side.

The simple equation of $X = T + eX$ has a parallel equation at the level of the variance or variability of a measure. That is, across a set of scores, we assume that:

$$\text{var (X)} = \text{var (T)} + \text{var (eX)}$$

In more human terms this means that the variability of your measure is the sum of the variability due to true score and the variability due to random error. This will have important implications when we consider some of the more advanced models for adjusting for errors in measurement. For one thing, it is a simple yet powerful model for measurement. It reminds us that most measurement has an error component. Second, true score theory is the foundation of reliability theory. A measure that has no random error is perfectly reliable; a measure that has no true score has zero reliability. Third, true score theory can be used in computer simulations as the basis for generating "observed" scores with certain known properties.

You should know that the true score model is not the only measurement model available. Measurement theorists continue to come up with more and more complex models that they think represent reality even better. But these models are complicated enough that they lie outside the boundaries of this document. In any event, true score theory should give you an idea of why measurement models are important at all and how they can be used as the basis for defining key research ideas.

MEASUREMENT ERROR

The true score theory is a good simple model for measurement, but it may not always be an accurate reflection of reality. In particular, it assumes that any observation is composed of the true value plus some random error value. But is that reasonable? What if all error is not random? Isn't it possible that some errors are systematic, that they hold across most or all of the members of a group? One way to deal with this notion is to revise the simple true score model by dividing the error component into two subcomponents, random error and systematic error. Here, we'll look at the differences between these two types of errors and try to diagnose their effects on our research.

Random Error

Random error is caused by any factors that randomly affect measurement of the variable across the sample. For instance, each person's mood can inflate or deflate their performance on any occasion. In a particular testing, some children may be feeling in a good mood and others may be depressed. If mood affects their performance on the measure, it may artificially inflate the observed scores for some children and artificially deflate them for others.

The important thing about random error is that it does not have any consistent effects across the entire sample. Instead, it pushes observed scores up or down randomly. This means that if we could see all of the random errors in a distribution they would have to sum to—there would be as many negative errors as positive ones. The important property of random error is that it adds variability to the data but does not affect average performance for the group. Because of this, random error is sometimes considered noise.

Systematic Error

Systematic error is caused by any factors that systematically affect measurement of the variable across the sample. For instance, if there is loud traffic going by just outside of a classroom where students are taking a test, this noise is liable to affect all of the children's scores—in this case, systematically lowering them. Unlike random error, systematic errors tend to be consistently either positive or negative—because of this, systematic error is sometimes considered to be bias in measurement.

Reducing Measurement Error

One thing you can do is to pilot test your instruments, getting feedback from your respondents regarding how easy or hard the measure was and information about how the testing environment affected their performance. Second, if you are gathering measures using people to collect the data you should make sure you train them thoroughly so that they aren't inadvertently introducing error. Third, when you collect the data for your study you should double-check the data thoroughly. All data entry for computer analysis should be "double-punched" and verified.

This means that you enter the data twice, the second time having your data entry machine check that you are typing the exact same data you did the first time. Fourth, you can use statistical procedures to adjust for measurement error. These range from rather simple formulas you can apply directly to your data to very complex modelling procedures for modelling the error and its effects. Finally, one of the best things you can do to deal with measurement errors, especially systematic errors, is to use multiple measures of the same construct. Especially if the different measures don't share the same systematic errors, you will be able to triangulate across the multiple measures and get a more accurate sense of what's going on.

Theory of Reliability

You learned in the Theory of Reliability that it's not possible to calculate reliability exactly. Instead, we have to estimate reliability, and this is always an imperfect endeavour. Here, we want to introduce the major reliability estimators and talk about their strengths and weaknesses.

There are four general classes of reliability estimates, each of which estimates reliability in a different way. They are:

— *Inter-Rater or Inter-Observer Reliability*: Used to assess the degree to which different raters/ observers give consistent estimates of the same phenomenon.

— *Test-Retest Reliability*: Used to assess the consistency of a measure from one time to another.

— *Parallel-Forms Reliability*: Used to assess the consistency of the results of two tests constructed in the same way from the same content domain.

— *Internal Consistency Reliability*: Used to assess the consistency of results across items within a test.

Let's discuss each of these in turn.

Inter-Rater Reliability

Whenever you use humans as a part of your measurement procedure, you have to worry about whether the results you get are reliable or consistent. People are notorious for their inconsistency. We are easily distractible. We get tired of doing repetitive tasks. We daydream. We misinterpret. So how do we determine whether two observers are being consistent in their observations? You probably should establish inter-rater reliability outside of the context of the measurement in your study.

After all, if you use data from your study to establish reliability, and you find that reliability is low, you're kind of stuck. Probably it's best to do this as a side study or pilot study. And, if your study goes on for a long time, you may want to reestablish inter-rater reliability from time to time to assure that your raters aren't changing. There are two major ways to actually estimate inter-rater reliability. If your measurement consists of categories—the raters are checking off which category each observation falls in—you can calculate the percent of agreement between the raters.

For instance, let's say you had 100 observations that were being rated by two raters. For each observation, the rater could check one of three categories. Imagine that on 86 of the 100 observations the raters checked the same category. In this case, the percent of agreement would be 86%. OK, it's a crude measure, but it does give an idea of how much agreement exists, and it works no matter how many categories are used for each observation. The other major way to estimate inter-rater reliability is appropriate when the measure is a continuous one. There, all you need to do is calculate the correlation between the ratings of the two observers.

For instance, they might be rating the overall level of activity in a classroom on a 1-to-7 scale. You could have them give their rating at regular time intervals. The correlation between these ratings would give you an estimate of the reliability or consistency between the raters. You might think of this type of reliability as "calibrating" the observers. There are other things you could do to encourage reliability between observers, even if you don't estimate it. For instance, we used to work in a psychiatric unit where every morning a nurse had to do a ten-item rating of each patient on the unit. Of course, we couldn't count on the same nurse being present every day, so we had to find a way to assure that any of the nurses would give comparable ratings.

The way we did it was to hold weekly "calibration" meetings where we would have all of the nurses ratings for several patients and discuss why they chose the specific values they did. If there were disagreements, the nurses would discuss them and attempt to come up with rules for deciding when they would give a "3" or a "4" for a rating on a specific item. Although this was not an estimate of reliability, it probably went a long way toward improving the reliability between raters.

Test-retest Reliability

We estimate test-retest reliability when we administer the same test to the same sample on two different occasions. This approach assumes that there is no substantial change in the construct being measured between the two occasions. The amount of time allowed between measures is critical. We know that if we measure the same thing twice that the correlation between the two observations will depend in part by how much time elapses between the two measurement occasions.

The shorter the time gap, the higher the correlation; the longer the time gap, the lower the correlation. This is because the two observations are related over time—the closer in time we get the more similar the factors that contribute to error. Since this correlation is the test-retest estimate of reliability, you can obtain considerably different estimates depending on the interval.

Parallel-forms Reliability

In parallel forms reliability you first have to create two parallel forms. One way to accomplish this is to create a large set of questions that address the same construct and then randomly divide the questions into two sets. You administer both instruments to the same sample of people. The correlation between the two parallel forms is the estimate of reliability. One major problem with this approach is that you have to be able to generate lots of items that reflect the same construct. This is often no easy feat. Furthermore, this approach makes the assumption that the randomly divided halves are parallel or equivalent. Even by chance this will sometimes not be the case.

The parallel forms approach is very similar to the split-half reliability described below. The major difference is that parallel forms are constructed so that the two forms can be used independent of each other and considered equivalent measures. For instance, we might be concerned about a testing threat to internal validity. If we use Form A for the pretest and Form B for the posttest, we minimise that problem. It would even be better if we randomly assign individuals to receive Form A or B on the pretest and then switch them on the posttest. With split-half reliability we have an instrument that we wish to use as a single measurement instrument and only develop randomly split halves for purposes of estimating reliability.

Internal Consistency Reliability

In internal consistency reliability estimation we use our single measurement instrument administered to a group of people on one occasion to estimate reliability. In effect we judge the reliability of the instrument by estimating how well the items that reflect the same construct yield similar results. We are looking at how consistent the results are for different items for the same construct within the measure. There are a wide variety of internal consistency measures that can be used.

Average Inter-item Correlation

The average inter-item correlation uses all of the items on our instrument that are designed to measure the same construct. We first compute the correlation between each pair of items. For example, if we have six items we will have 15 different item pairings. The average interitem correlation is simply the average or mean of all these correlations.

Split-Half Reliability

In split-half reliability we randomly divide all items that purport to measure the same construct into two sets. We administer the entire instrument to a sample of people and calculate the total score for each randomly divided half. The split-half reliability estimate is simply the correlation between these two total scores.

Comparison of Reliability Estimators

Each of the reliability estimators has certain advantages and disadvantages. Inter-rater reliability is one of the best ways to estimate reliability when your measure is an observation. However, it requires multiple raters or observers. As an alternative, you could look at the correlation of ratings of the same single observer repeated on two different occasions. For example, let's say you collected videotapes of child-mother interactions and had a rater code the videos for how often the mother smiled at the child. To establish inter-rater reliability you could take a sample of videos and have two raters code them independently.

To estimate test-retest reliability you could have a single rater code the same videos on two different occasions. You might use the inter-rater approach especially if you were interested in using a team of raters and you wanted to establish that they yielded consistent results. If you get a suitably high inter-rater reliability you could then justify allowing them to work independently on coding different videos. You might use the test-retest approach when you only have a single rater and don't want to train any others. On the other hand, in some studies it is reasonable to do both to help establish the reliability of the raters or observers.

The parallel forms estimator is typically only used in situations where you intend to use the two forms as alternate measures of the same thing. Both the parallel forms and all of the internal consistency estimators have one major constraint—you have to have multiple items designed to measure the same construct. This is relatively easy to achieve in certain contexts like achievement testing, but for more complex or subjective constructs this can be a real challenge. If you do have lots of items, Cronbach's Alpha tends to be the most frequently used estimate of internal consistency.

The test-retest estimator is especially feasible in most experimental and quasi-experimental designs that use a no-treatment control group. In these designs you always have a control group that is measured on two occasions (pretest and posttest). The main problem with this approach is that you don't have any information about reliability until you collect the posttest and, if the reliability estimate is low, you're pretty much sunk. Each of the reliability estimators will give a different value for reliability.

In general, the test-retest and inter-rater reliability estimates will be lower in value than the parallel forms and internal consistency ones because they involve measuring at different times or with different raters. Since reliability estimates are often used in statistical analyses of quasi-experimental designs, the fact that different estimates can differ considerably makes the analysis even more complex.

LEVELS OF MEASUREMENT

The level of measurement refers to the relationship among the values that are assigned to the attributes for a variable. What does that mean? Begin with the idea of the variable, in this example "party affiliation." That variable has a number of attributes. Let's assume that in this particular election context the only relevant attributes are "republican", "democrat", and "independent". For purposes of analysing the results of this variable, we arbitrarily assign the values 1, 2 and 3 to the three attributes.

The level of measurement describes the relationship among these three values. In this case, we simply are using the numbers as shorter placeholders for the lengthier text terms. We don't assume that higher values mean "more" of something and lower numbers signify "less". We don't assume the value of 2 means that democrats are twice something that republicans are. We don't assume that republicans are in first place or have the highest priority just because they have the value of 1. In this case, we only use the values as a shorter name for the attribute. Here, we would describe the level of measurement as "nominal".

Importance

First, knowing the level of measurement helps you decide how to interpret the data from that variable. When you know that a measure is nominal, then you know that the numerical values are just short codes for the longer names. Second, knowing the level of measurement helps you decide what statistical analysis is appropriate on the values that were assigned. If a measure is nominal, then you know that you would never average the data values or do a t-test on the data.

There are typically four levels of measurement that are defined:

— Nominal.

— Ordinal.

— Interval.

— Ratio.

In nominal measurement the numerical values just "name" the attribute uniquely. No ordering of the cases is implied. For example, jersey numbers in basketball are measures at the nominal level. A player with number 30 is not more of anything than a player with number 15, and is certainly not twice whatever number 15 is. In ordinal measurement the attributes can be rank-ordered. Here, distances between attributes do not have any meaning. For example, on a survey you might code Educational Attainment as 0=less than H.S.; 1=some H.S.; 2=H.S. degree; 3=some college; 4=college degree; 5=post college. In this measure, higher numbers mean more education.

In interval measurement the distance between attributes does have meaning. For example, when we measure temperature (in Fahrenheit), the distance from 30-40 is same as distance from 70-80. The interval between values is interpretable. Because of this, it makes sense to compute an average of an interval variable, where it doesn't make sense to do so for ordinal scales. But note that in interval measurement ratios don't make any sense—80 degrees is not twice as hot as 40 degrees (although the attribute value is twice as large).

Finally, in ratio measurement there is always an absolute zero that is meaningful. This means that you can construct a meaningful fraction with a ratio variable. Weight is a ratio variable. In applied social research most "count" variables are ratio, for example, the number of clients in past six months. Because you can have zero clients and because it is meaningful to say that "...we had twice as many clients in the past six months as we did in the previous six months." It's important to recognise that there is a hierarchy implied in the level of measurement idea. At lower levels of measurement, assumptions tend to be less restrictive and data analyses tend to be less sensitive. At each level up the hierarchy, the current level includes all of the qualities of the one below it and adds something new. In general, it is desirable to have a higher level of measurement rather than a lower one.

7

Survey Research

Survey research is one of the most important areas of measurement in applied social research. The broad area of survey research encompasses any measurement procedures that involve asking questions of respondents. A "survey" can be anything form a short paper-and-pencil feedback form to an intensive one-on-one in-depth interview.

TYPES OF SURVEYS

Surveys can be divided into two broad categories: the questionnaire and the interview. Questionnaires are usually paper-and-pencil instruments that the respondent completes. Interviews are completed by the interviewer based on the respondent says. Sometimes, it's hard to tell the difference between a questionnaire and an interview. For instance, some people think that questionnaires always ask short closed-ended questions while interviews always ask broad open-ended ones. But you will see questionnaires with open-ended questions and there will often be a series of closed-ended questions asked in an interview.

Survey research has changed dramatically in the last ten years. We have automated telephone surveys that use random dialing methods. There are computerised kiosks in public places that allows people to ask for input. A whole new variation of group interview has evolved as focus group methodology. Increasingly, survey research is tightly integrated with the delivery of service. Your hotel room has a survey on the desk. Your waiter presents a short customer satisfaction survey with your check. You get a call for an interview several days after your last call to a computer company for technical assistance. You're asked to complete a short survey when you visit a web site. Here, we'll describe the major types of questionnaires and interviews, keeping in mind that technology is leading to rapid evolution of methods. We'll discuss the relative advantages and disadvantages of these different survey types in Advantages and Disadvantages of Survey Methods.

Questionnaires

When most people think of questionnaires, they think of the mail survey. All of us have, at one time or another, received a questionnaire in the mail. There are many advantages to mail surveys. They are relatively inexpensive to administer. You can send the exact same instrument to a wide number of people. They allow the respondent to fill it out at their own convenience. But there are some disadvantages as well. Response rates from mail surveys are often very low. And, mail questionnaires are not the best vehicles for asking for detailed written responses.

A second type is the group administered questionnaire. A sample of respondents is brought together and asked to respond to a structured sequence of questions. Traditionally, questionnaires were administered in group settings for convenience. The researcher could give the questionnaire to those who were present and be fairly sure that there would be a high response rate. If the respondents were unclear about the meaning of a question they could ask for clarification. And, there were often organisational settings where it was relatively easy to assemble the group.

In the group administered questionnaire, each respondent is handed an instrument and asked to complete it while in the room. Each respondent completes an instrument. In the group interview or focus group, the interviewer facilitates the session. People work as a group, listening to each other's comments and answering the questions. Someone takes notes for the entire group—people don't complete an interview individually. A less familiar type of questionnaire is the household drop-off survey. In this approach, a researcher goes to the respondent's home or business and hands the respondent the instrument.

In some cases, the respondent is asked to mail it back or the interview returns to pick it up. This approach attempts to blend the advantages of the mail survey and the group administered questionnaire. Like the mail survey, the respondent can work on the instrument in private, when it's convenient. Like the group administered questionnaire, the interviewer makes personal contact with the respondent—they don't just send an impersonal survey instrument. And, the respondent can ask questions about the study and get clarification on what is to be done. Generally, this would be expected to increase the percent of people who are willing to respond.

Interviews

Interviews are a far more personal form of research than questionnaires. In the personal interview, the interviewer works directly with the respondent. Unlike with mail surveys, the interviewer has the opportunity to probe or ask follow-up questions. And, interviews are generally easier for the respondent, especially if what is sought is opinions or impressions. Interviews can be very time consuming and they are resource intensive. The interviewer is considered a part of the measurement instrument and interviewers have to be well trained in how to respond to any contingency.

Almost everyone is familiar with the telephone interview. Telephone interviews enable a researcher to gather information rapidly. Most of the major public opinion polls that are reported were based on telephone interviews. Like personal interviews, they allow for some personal contact between the interviewer and the respondent. And, they allow the interviewer to ask follow-up questions. But they also have some major disadvantages. Many people don't have publicly-listed telephone numbers. Some don't have telephones. People often don't like the intrusion of a call to their homes. And, telephone interviews have to be relatively short or people will feel imposed upon.

SELECTING THE TYPE OF SURVEY METHOD

Selecting the type of survey you are going to use is one of the most critical decisions in many social research contexts. You'll see that there are very few simple rules that will make the decision for you—you have to use your judgment to balance the advantages and disadvantages of different survey types.

Population Issues

The first set of considerations have to do with the population and its accessibility.

For some populations, you have a complete listing of the units that will be sampled. For others, such a list is difficult or impossible to compile. For instance, there are complete listings of registered voters or person with active drivers licenses. But no one keeps a complete list of homeless people. If you are doing a study that requires input from homeless persons, you are very likely going to need to go and find the respondents personally. In such contexts, you can pretty much rule out the idea of mail surveys or telephone interviews.

Questionnaires require that your respondents can read. While this might seem initially like a reasonable assumption for many adult populations, we know from recent research that the instance of adult illiteracy is alarmingly high. And, even if your respondents can read to some degree, your questionnaire may contain difficult or technical vocabulary. Clearly, there are some populations that you would expect to be illiterate. Young children would not be good targets for questionnaires.

We live in a multilingual world. Virtually every society has members who speak other than the predominant language. Some countries are officially multilingual. And, our increasingly global economy requires us to do research that spans countries and language groups. Can you produce multiple versions of your questionnaire? For mail instruments, can you know in advance the language your respondent speaks, or do you send multiple translations of your instrument? Can you be confident that important connotations in your instrument are not culturally specific? Could some of the important nuances get lost in the process of translating your questions?

People who do research on immigration issues have a difficult methodological problem. They often need to speak with undocumented immigrants or people who may be able to identify others who are. Why would we expect those respondents to cooperate? Although the researcher may mean no harm, the respondents are at considerable risk legally if information they divulge should get into the hand of the authorities. The same can be said for any target group that is engaging in illegal or unpopular activities.

· Is your population of interest dispersed over too broad a geographic range for you to study feasibly with a personal interview? It may be possible for you to send a mail instrument to a nationwide sample. You may be able to conduct phone interviews with them. But it will almost certainly be less feasible to do research that requires interviewers to visit directly with respondents if they are widely dispersed.

Important Sampling Issues

The sample is the actual group you will have to contact in some way. There are several important sampling issues you need to consider when doing survey research.

— What data is available?

What information do you have about your sample? Do you know their current addresses? Their current phone numbers? Are your contact lists up to date?

— Can respondents be found?

Can your respondents be located? Some people are very busy. Some travel a lot. Some work the night shift. Even if you have an accurate phone or address, you may not be able to locate or make contact with your sample.

— Who is the respondent?

Who is the respondent in your study? Let's say you draw a sample of households in a small city. A household is not a respondent. Do you want to interview a specific individual? Do you want to talk only to the "head of household"? Are you willing to talk to any member of the household? Do you state that you will speak to the first adult member of the household who opens the door? What if that person is unwilling to be interviewed but someone else in the house is willing? How do you deal with multi-family households? Similar problems arise when you sample groups, agencies, or companies. Can you survey any member of the organisation? Or, do you only want to speak to the Director of Human Resources? What if the person you would like to interview is unwilling or unable to participate? Do you use another member of the organisation?

— Can all members of population be sampled?

If you have an incomplete list of the population you may not be able to sample every member of the population. Lists of various groups are extremely hard to keep up to date. People move or change their names. Even though they are on your sampling frame listing, you may not be able to get to them. And, it's possible they are not even on the list.

— Are response rates likely to be a problem?

Even if you are able to solve all of the other population and sampling problems, you still have to deal with the issue of response rates. Some members of your sample will simply refuse to respond. Others have the best of intentions, but can't seem to find the time to send in your questionnaire by the due date. Still others misplace the instrument or forget about the appointment for an interview. Low response rates are among the most difficult of problems in survey research. They can ruin an otherwise well-designed survey effort.

Question Issues

Sometimes the nature of what you want to ask respondents will determine the type of survey you select.

— What types of questions can be asked?

Are you going to be asking personal questions? Are you going to need to get lots of detail in the responses? Can you anticipate the most frequent or important types of responses and develop reasonable closed-ended questions?

— How complex will the questions be?

Sometimes you are dealing with a complex subject or topic. The questions you want to ask are going to have multiple parts. You may need to branch to sub-questions.

— Will screening questions be needed?

A screening question may be needed to determine whether the respondent is qualified to answer your question of interest. For instance, you wouldn't want to ask someone their opinions about a specific computer programme without first "screening" them to find out whether they have any experience using the programme. Sometimes you have to screen on several variables. The more complicated the screening, the less likely it is that you can rely on paper-and-pencil instruments without confusing the respondent.

— Can question sequence be controlled?

Is your survey one where you can construct in advance a reasonable sequence of questions? Or, are you doing an initial exploratory study where you may need to ask lots of follow-up questions that you can't easily anticipate?

— Will lengthy questions be asked?

If your subject-matter is complicated, you may need to give the respondent some detailed background for a question. Can you reasonably expect your respondent to sit still long enough in a phone interview to ask your question?

— Will long response scales be used?

If you are asking people about the different computer equipment they use, you may have to have a lengthy response list. Clearly, it may be difficult to ask about each of these in a short phone interview.

Content Issues

The content of your study can also pose challenges for the different survey types you might utilise.

— Can the respondents be expected to know about the issue?

If the respondent does not keep up with the news, they may not even know about the news issue you want to ask them about. Or, if you want to do a study of family finances and you are talking to the spouse who doesn't pay the bills on a regular basis, they may not have the information to answer your questions.

— Will respondent need to consult records?

Even if the respondent understands what you're asking about, you may need to allow them to consult their records in order to get an accurate answer. For instance, if you ask them how much money they spent on food in the past month, they may need to look up their personal check and credit card records. In this case, you don't want to be involved in an interview where they would have to go look things up while they keep you waiting.

Bias Issues

People come to the research endeavour with their own sets of biases and prejudices. Sometimes, these biases will be less of a problem with certain types of survey approaches.

— Can social desirability be avoided?

Respondents generally want to "look good" in the eyes of others. None of us likes to look like we don't know an answer. We don't want to say anything that would be embarrassing. If you ask people about information that may put them in this kind of position, they may not tell you the truth, or they may "spin" the response so that it makes them look better. This may be more of a problem in an interview situation where they are face-to face or on the phone with a live interviewer.

— Can interviewer distortion and subversion be controlled?

Interviewers may distort an interview as well. They may not ask questions that make them uncomfortable. They may not listen carefully to respondents on topics for which they have strong opinions. They may make the judgment that they already know what the respondent would say to a question based on their prior responses, even though that may not be true.

— Can false respondents be avoided?

With mail surveys it may be difficult to know who actually responded. Did the head of household complete the survey or someone else? Did the CEO actually give the responses or instead pass the task off to a subordinate? Is the person you're speaking with on the phone actually who they say they are? At least with personal interviews, you have a reasonable chance of knowing who you are speaking with. In mail surveys or phone interviews, this may not be the case.

Administrative Issues

Last, but certainly not least, you have to consider the feasibility of the survey method for your study.

— Costs.

Cost is often the major determining factor in selecting survey type. You might prefer to do personal interviews, but can't justify the high cost of training and paying for the interviewers. You may prefer to send out an extensive mailing but can't afford the postage to do so.

— Facilities.

Do you have the facilities to process and manage your study? In phone interviews, do you have well-equipped phone surveying facilities? For focus groups, do you have a comfortable and accessible room to host the group? Do you have the equipment needed to record and transcribe responses?

— Time.

Some types of surveys take longer than others. Do you need responses immediately (as in an overnight public opinion poll)? Have you budgeted enough time for your study to send out mail surveys and follow-up reminders, and to get the responses back by mail? Have you allowed for enough time to get enough personal interviews to justify that approach?

— Personnel.

Different types of surveys make different demands of personnel. Interviews require interviewers who are motivated and well-trained. Group administered surveys require people who are trained in group facilitation. Some studies may be in a technical area that requires some degree of expertise in the interviewer.

Clearly, there are lots of issues to consider when you are selecting which type of survey you wish to use in your study. And there is no clear and easy way to make this decision in many contexts. There may not be one approach which is clearly the best. You may have to make tradeoffs of advantages and disadvantages. There is judgement involved. Two expert researchers may, for the very same problem or issue, select entirely different survey methods. But, if you select a method that isn't appropriate or doesn't fit the context, you can doom a study before you even begin designing the instruments or questions themselves.

CONSTRUCTING THE SURVEY

Constructing a survey instrument is an art in itself. There are numerous small decisions that must be made—about content, wording, format, placement—that can have important consequences for your entire study. While there's no one perfect way to accomplish this job, we do have lots of advice to offer that might increase your chances of developing a better final product.

First of all you'll learn about the two major types of surveys that exist, the questionnaire and the interview and the different varieties of each. Then you'll see how to write questions for surveys. There are three areas involved in writing a question:

— Determining the question content, scope and purpose.

— Choosing the response format that you use for collecting information from the respondent.

— Figuring out how to word the question to get at the issue of interest.

Finally, once you have your questions written, there is the issue of how best to place them in your survey. You'll see that although there are many aspects of survey construction that are just common sense, if you are not careful you can make critical errors that have dramatic effects on your results.

TYPES OF QUESTIONS

Survey questions can be divided into two broad types: structured and unstructured. From an instrument design point of view, the structured questions pose the greater difficulties. From a content perspective, it may actually be more difficult to write good unstructured questions. For each question in your survey, you should ask yourself how well it addresses the content you are trying to get at. Here are some content-related questions you can ask about your survey questions.

Examine each question to see if you need to ask it at all and if you need to ask it at the level of detail you currently have. You should think about splitting each of the following questions into two separate ones. You can often spot these kinds of problems by looking for the conjunction "and" in your question.

Another reason you might need more than one question is that the question you ask does not cover all possibilities. For instance, if you ask about earnings, the respondent might not mention all income. Or, if you ask the respondents if they're in favour of public TV, they might not understand that you're asking generally. They may not be in favour of public TV for themselves, but might favour it very much for their children. You might be better off asking two questions, one for their own viewing and one for other members of their household.

Sometimes you need to ask additional questions because your question does not give you enough context to interpret the answer. For instance, if you ask about attitudes towards Muslims, can you interpret this without finding out about their attitudes towards religion in general, or other religious groups? At times, you need to ask additional questions because your question does not determine the intensity of the respondent's attitude or belief. For example, if they say they support public TV, you probably should also ask them whether they ever watch it or if they would be willing to have their tax dollars spent on it. It's one thing for a respondent to tell you they support something. But the intensity of that response is greater if they are willing to back their sentiment of support with their behaviour.

Look at each question in your survey to see whether the respondent is likely to have the necessary information to be able to answer the question. For example, let's say you want to ask the question.

The respondent won't be able to answer this question if they have no idea about that question. In surveys of television viewing, you cannot expect that the respondent can answer questions about shows they have never watched. You should ask a filter question first before asking them their opinions about it. Sometimes we ask our questions too generally and the information we obtain is more difficult to interpret. For example, let's say you want to find out respondent's opinions about a specific book. You could ask them

You can err in the other direction as well by being too specific. For instance, if you ask someone to list the televisions programme they liked best in the past week, you could get a very different answer than if you asked them which show they've enjoyed most over the past year. Perhaps a show they don't usually like had a great episode in the past week, or their show was preempted by another programme. One danger in question-writing is that your own biases and blind-spots may affect the wording. For instance, you might generally be in favour of tax cuts. If you ask a question like:

For each question on your survey, ask yourself whether the respondent will have any difficulty answering the question truthfully. If there is some reason why they may not, consider rewording the question. For instance, some people are sensitive about answering questions about their exact age or income. In this case, you might give them response brackets to choose from. Sometimes even bracketed responses won't be enough. Some people do not like to share how much money they give to charitable causes. No matter how you word the question, they would not be likely to tell you their contribution rate. But sometimes you can do this by posing the question in terms of a hypothetical projective respondent.

In this case, you might get reasonable estimates if you ask the respondent how much money "people you know" typically give in a year to charitable causes. Finally, you can sometimes dispense with asking a question at all if you can obtain the answer unobtrusively. If you are interested in finding out what magazines the respondent reads, you might instead tell them you are collecting magazines for a recycling drive and ask if they have any old ones to donate.

RESPONSE FORMAT

The response format is how you collect the answer from the respondent. Let's start with a simple distinction between what we'll call unstructured response formats and structured response formats.

Structured Response Formats

Structured formats help the respondent to respond more easily and help the researcher to accumulate and summarise responses more efficiently. But, they can also constrain the respondent and limit the researcher's ability to understand what the respondent really means. There are many different structured response formats, each with its own strengths and weaknesses. We'll review the major ones here.

Fill-In-The-Blank: One of the simplest response formats is a blank line. A blank line can be used for a number of different response types. For instance:

Please enter your gender:

— Male.

— Female.

Here, the respondent would probably put a check mark or an X next to the response. This is also an example of a dichotomous response, because it only has two possible values. Other common dichotomous responses are True/False and Yes/No. Here's another common use of a fill-in-the-blank response format:

Please enter your preference for the following candidates where '1' = your first choice, '2' = your second choice, and so on.

— Mr. Obama

— Mrs. Clinton

— Mr. Al Gore.

— Mr. Colin Powell.

In this example, the respondent writes a number in each blank. Notice that here, we expect the respondent to place a number on every blank, whereas in the previous example, we expect to respondent to choose only one. Then, of course, there's the classic:

NAME: ______________________________

And here's the same fill-in-the-blank response item in web format:

NAME:

Of course, there's always the classic fill-in-the-blank test item:

One of Mrs. Indira Gandhi's most famous speeches, the Address, only lasted a few minutes when delivered.

Check The Answer: The respondent places a check next to the response(s). The simplest form would be the example given above where we ask the person to indicate their gender. Sometimes, we supply a box that the person can fill in with an 'X', which is sort of a variation on the check mark. Here's a web version of the checkbox:

You have to be careful when you analyse data from a multi-option variable. Because the respondent can select any of the options, you have to treat this type of variable in your analysis as though each option is a separate variable. For instance, for each option we would normally enter either a '0' if the respondent did not check it or a '1' if the respondent did check it. For the example above, if the respondent had only a modem and CD-ROM drive, we would enter the sequence 1, 0, 1, 0, 0. There is a very important reason why you should code this variable as either 0 or 1 when you enter the data.

If you do, and you want to determine what percent of your sample has a modem, all you have to do is compute the average of the 0's and 1's for the modem variable. For instance, if you have 10 respondents and only 3 have a modem, the average would be 3/10 =.30 or 30%, which is the percent who checked that item.

The example above is also a good example of a checklist item. Whenever you use a checklist, you want to be sure that you ask the following questions:

— Are all of the alternatives covered?

— Is the list of reasonable length?

— Is the wording impartial?

— Is the form of the response easy, uniform?

Sometimes you may not be sure that you have covered all of the possible responses in a checklist. If that is the case, you should probably allow the respondent to write in any other options that may apply. Sometimes the respondent is asked to circle an item to indicate their response. Usually we are asking them to circle a number. In computer contexts, it's not feasible to have respondents circle a response.

Unstructured Response Formats

Generally, unstructured response formats is written text. If the respondent writes down text as the response, you've got an unstructured response format. These can vary from short comment boxes to the transcript of an interview. In almost every short questionnaire, there's one or more short text field questions. One of the most frequent goes something like this:

Actually, there's really not much more to text-based response formats of this type than writing the prompt and allowing enough space for a reasonable response. Transcripts are an entirely different matter. There, the transcriber has to decide whether to transcribe every word or only record major ideas, thoughts, quotes, etc.

In detailed transcriptions, you may also need to distinguish different speakers and have a standard convention for indicating comments about what's going on in the interview, including non-conversational events that take place and thoughts of the interviewer.

Question Wording

One of the major difficulty in writing good survey questions is getting the wording right. Even slight wording differences can confuse the respondent or lead to incorrect interpretations of the question. The survey author has to always be on the lookout for questions that could be misunderstood or confusing. For instance, if you ask a person for their nationality, it might not be clear what you want. Or, if you ask for marital status, do you want someone to say simply that they are either married or no married? Or, do you want more detail ? Some terms are just to vague to be useful. For instance, if you ask a question about the "mass media," what do you mean? The newspapers? Radio? Television?

Sometimes we don't stop to consider how a question will appear from the respondent's point-of-view. We don't think about the assumptions behind our questions. For instance, if you ask what social class someone's in, you assume that they know what social class is and that they think of themselves as being in one. In this kind of case, you may need to use a filter question first to determine whether either of these assumptions is true. Whenever you use the words "will", "could", "might", or "may" in a question, you might suspect that the question asks a time-related question. Be sure that, if it does, you have specified the time frame precisely. For instance, you might ask:

With a change of just a few words, a question can go from being relatively impersonal to probing into your private perspectives. Consider the following three questions, each of which asks about the respondent's satisfaction with working conditions:

— Are working conditions satisfactory or not satisfactory in the plant where you work?

— Do you feel that working conditions satisfactory or not satisfactory in the plant where you work?

— Are you personally satisfied with working conditions in the plant where you work?

The first question is stated from a fairly detached, objective viewpoint. The second asks how you "feel." The last asks whether you are "personally satisfied." Be sure the questions in your survey are at an appropriate level for your context. And, be sure there is consistency in this across questions in your survey.

There are times when asking a question too directly may be too threatening or disturbing for respondents. For instance, consider a study where you want to discuss battlefield experiences with former soldiers who experienced trauma. Examine the following three question options:

— How did you feel about being in the war?

— How well did the equipment hold up in the field?

— How well were new recruits trained?

The first question may be too direct. For this population it may elicit powerful negative emotions based on their recollections. The second question is a less direct one. It asks about equipment in the field, but, for this population, may also lead the discussion toward more difficult issues to discuss directly. The last question is probably the least direct and least threatening. Bashing the new recruits is standard protocol in almost any social context.

The question is likely to get the respondent talking, recounting anecdotes, without eliciting much stress. Of course, all of this may simply be begging the question. If you are doing a study where the respondents may experience high levels of stress because of the questions you ask, you should reconsider the ethics of doing the study.

The nuances of language guarantee that the task of the question writer will be endlessly complex. Without trying to generate an exhaustive list, here are a few other questions to keep in mind:

— Does the question contain difficult or unclear terminology?

— Does the question make each alternative explicit?

— Is the wording objectionable?

— Is the wording loaded or slanted?

Question Placement

One of the most difficult tasks facing the survey designer involves the ordering of questions. Which topics should be introduced early in the survey, and which later? If you leave your most important questions until the end, you may find that your respondents are too tired to give them the kind of attention you would like. If you introduce them too early, they may not yet be ready to address the topic, especially if it is a difficult or disturbing one. There are no easy answers to these problems—you have to use your judgement. Whenever you think about question placement, consider the following questions:

— Is the answer influenced by prior questions?

— Does question come too early or too late to arouse interest?

— Does the question receive sufficient attention?

Opening Questions

Just as in other aspects of life, first impressions are important in survey work. The first few questions you ask will determine the tone for the survey, and can help put your respondent at ease. With that in mind, the opening few questions should, in general, be easy to answer. You might start with some simple descriptive questions that will get the respondent rolling. You should never begin your survey with sensitive or threatening questions.

Sensitive Questions

In much of our social research, we have to ask respondents about difficult or uncomfortable subjects. Before asking such questions, you should attempt to develop some trust or rapport with the respondent. Often, preceding the sensitive questions with some easier warm-up ones will help. But, you have to make sure that the sensitive material does not come up abruptly or appear unconnected with the rest of the survey. It is often helpful to have a transition sentence between sections of your instrument to give the respondent some idea of the kinds of questions that are coming. For instance, you might lead into a section on personal material with the transition.

Checklist of Considerations

There are lots of conventions or rules-of-thumb in the survey design business. Here's a checklist of some of the most important items. You can use this checklist to review your instrument:

— Start with easy, nonthreatening questions.

— Put more difficult, threatening questions near end.

— Never start a mail survey with an open-ended question.

— For historical demographics, follow chronological order.

— Ask about one topic at a time.

— When switching topics, use a transition.

— Reduce response set.

— For filter or contingency questions, make a flowchart.

Golden Rule

You are imposing in the life of your respondent. You are asking for their time, their attention, their trust, and often, for personal information.

INTERVIEWS

Interviews are among the most challenging and rewarding forms of measurement. They require a personal sensitivity and adaptability as well as the ability to stay within the bounds of the designed protocol.

Interviewer

The interviewer is really the "jack-of-all-trades" in survey research. The interviewer's role is complex and multifaceted. It includes the following tasks:

— Locate and enlist cooperation of respondents.

The interviewer has to find the respondent. In door-to-door surveys, this means being able to locate specific addresses. Often, the interviewer has to work at the least desirable times because that's when respondents are most readily available.

— Motivate respondents to do good job.

If the interviewer does not take the work seriously, why would the respondent? The interviewer has to be motivated and has to be able to communicate that motivation to the respondent. Often, this means that the interviewer has to be convinced of the importance of the research.

— Clarify any confusion/concerns.

Interviewers have to be able to think on their feet. Respondents may raise objections or concerns that were not anticipated. The interviewer has to be able to respond candidly and informatively.

— Observe quality of responses.

Whether the interview is personal or over the phone, the interviewer is in the best position to judge the quality of the information that is being received. Even a verbatim transcript will not adequately convey how seriously the respondent took the task, or any gestures or body language that were evident.

— Conduct a good interview.

Last, and certainly not least, the interviewer has to conduct a good interview! Every interview has a life of its own. Some respondents are motivated and attentive, others are distracted or disinterested. The interviewer also has good or bad days. Assuring a consistently high-quality interview is a challenge that requires constant effort.

Training the Interviewers

One of the most important aspects of any interview study is the training of the interviewers themselves. In many ways the interviewers are your measures, and the quality of the results is totally in their hands. Even in small studies involving only a single researcher-interviewer, it is important to organise in detail and rehearse the interviewing process before beginning the formal study.

Here are some of the major topics that should be included in interviewer training:

— Describe the entire study.

Interviewers need to know more than simply how to conduct the interview itself. They should learn about the background for the study, previous work that has been done, and why the study is important.

— State who is sponsor of research.

Interviewers need to know who they are working for. They—and their respondents—have a right to know not just what agency or company is conducting the research, but also, who is paying for the research.

— Teach enough about survey research.

While you seldom have the time to teach a full course on survey research methods, the interviewers need to know enough that they respect the survey method and are motivated. Sometimes it may not be apparent why a question or set of questions was asked in a particular way. The interviewers will need to understand the rationale for how the instrument was constructed.

— Explain the sampling logic and process.

Naive interviewers may not understand why sampling is so important. They may wonder why you go through all the difficulties of selecting the sample so carefully. You will have to explain that sampling is the basis for the conclusions that will be reached and for the degree to which your study will be useful.

— Explain interviewer bias.

Interviewers need to know the many ways that

they can inadvertently bias the results. And, they need to understand why it is important that they not bias the study. This is especially a problem when you are investigating political or moral issues on which people have strongly held convictions. While the interviewer may think they are doing good for society by slanting results in favour of what they believe, they need to recognise that doing so could jeopardize the entire study in the eyes of others.

— "Walk through" the interview.

When you first introduce the interview, it's a good idea to walk through the entire protocol so the interviewers can get an idea of the various parts or phases and how they interrelate.

— Explain respondent selection procedures, including.

- Reading maps.

  It's astonishing how many adults don't know how to follow directions on a map. In personal interviews, the interviewer may need to locate respondents who are spread over a wide geographic area. And, they often have to navigate by night in neighbourhoods they're not familiar with. Teaching basic map reading skills and confirming that the interviewers can follow maps is essential.

- Identifying households.

  In many studies it is impossible in advance to say whether every sample household meets the sampling requirements for the study. In your study, you may want to interview only people who live in single family homes. It may be impossible to distinguish townhouses and apartment buildings in your sampling frame.

The interviewer must know how to identify the appropriate target household.

- Identify respondents.

  Just as with households, many studies require respondents who meet specific criteria. For instance, your study may require that you speak with a male head-of-household between the ages of 30 and 40 who has children under 18 living in the same household. It may be impossible to obtain statistics in advance to target such respondents. The interviewer may have to ask a series of filtering questions before determining whether the respondent meets the sampling needs.

— Rehearse interview.

You should probably have several rehearsal sessions with the interviewer team. You might even videotape rehearsal interviews to discuss how the trainees responded in difficult situations. The interviewers should be very familiar with the entire interview before ever facing a respondent.

— Explain supervision.

In most interview studies, the interviewers will work under the direction of a supervisor. In some contexts, the supervisor may be a faculty advisor; in others, they may be the "boss." In order to assure the quality of the responses, the supervisor may have to observe a subsample of interviews, listen in on phone interviews, or conduct follow-up assessments of interviews with the respondents. This can be very threatening to the interviewers. You need to develop an atmosphere where everyone on the research team—interviewers and supervisors—feel like they're working together towards a common end.

— Explain scheduling.

The interviewers have to understand the demands being made on their schedules and why these are important to the study. In some studies it will be imperative to conduct the entire set of interviews within a certain time period. In most studies, it's important to have the interviewers available when it's convenient for the respondents, not necessarily the interviewer.

Interviewer's Kit

It's important that interviewers have all of the materials they need to do a professional job. Usually, you will want to assemble an interviewer kit that can be easily carried and includes all of the important materials such as:

— A "professional-looking" 3-ring notebook (this might even have the logo of the company or organisation conducting the interviews).

— Maps.

— Sufficient copies of the survey instrument.

— Official identification.

— A cover letter from the Principal Investigator or Sponsor.

— A phone number the respondent can call to verify the interviewer's authenticity.

Interview Process

So all the preparation is complete, the training done, the interviewers ready to proceed, their "kits" in hand. It's finally time to do an actual interview. Each interview is unique, like a small work of art. Each interview has its own ebb and flow—its own pace. To the outsider, an interview looks like a fairly standard, simple, prosaic effort. But to the interviewer, it can be filled with special nuances and interpretations that aren't often immediately apparent. Every interview includes some common components.

There's the opening, where the interviewer gains entry and establishes the rapport and tone for what follows. There's the middle game, the heart of the process, that consists of the protocol of questions and the improvisations of the probe. And finally, there's the endgame, the wrap-up, where the interviewer and respondent establish a sense of closure. Whether it's a two-minute phone interview or a personal interview that spans hours, the interview is a bit of theater, a mini-drama that involves real lives in real time.

Opening Remarks

In many ways, the interviewer has the same initial problem that a salesperson has. You have to get the respondent's attention initially for a long enough period that you can sell them on the idea of participating in the study. Many of the remarks here assume an interview that is being conducted at a respondent's residence. But the analogies to other interview contexts should be straightforward.

— Gaining entry.

The first thing the interviewer must do is gain entry. Several factors can enhance the prospects. Probably the most important factor is your initial appearance. The interviewer needs to dress professionally and in a manner that will be comfortable to the respondent. In some contexts a business suit and briefcase may be appropriate. In others, it may intimidate. The way the interviewer appears initially to the respondent has to communicate some simple messages—that you're trustworthy, honest, and non-threatening. Cultivating a manner of professional confidence, the sense that the respondent has nothing to worry about because you know what you're doing—is a difficult skill to teach and an indispensable skill for achieving initial entry.

— Doorstep technique.

You're standing on the doorstep and someone has opened the door, even if only halfway. You need to smile. You need to be brief. State why you are there and suggest what you would like the respondent to do. Don't ask—suggest what you want.

— Introduction.

If you've gotten this far without having the door slammed in your face, chances are you will be able to get an interview. Without waiting for the respondent to ask questions, you should move to introducing yourself. You should have this part of the process memorised so you can deliver the essential information in 20-30 seconds at most. State your name and the name of the organisation you represent. Show your identification badge and the letter that introduces you. You want to have as legitimate an appearance as possible. If you have a three-ring binder or clipboard with the logo of your organisation, you should have it out and visible. You should assume that the respondent will be interested in participating in your important study—assume that you will be doing an interview here.

— Explaining the study.

At this point, you've been invited to come in (After

all, you're standing there in the cold, holding an assortment of materials, clearly displaying your credentials, and offering the respondent the chance to participate in an interview—to many respondents, it's a rare and exciting event. They hardly ever get asked their views about anything, and yet they know that important decisions are made all the time based on input from others.). Or, the respondent has continued to listen long enough that you need to move onto explaining the study. There are three rules to this critical explanation: 1) Keep it short; 2) Keep it short; and 3) Keep it short! The respondent doesn't have to or want to know all of the neat nuances of this study, how it came about, how you convinced your thesis committee to buy into it, and so on. You should have a one or two sentence description of the study memorised. No big words. No jargon. No detail. There will be more than enough time for that later. This is the "25 words or less" description. What you should spend some time on is assuring the respondent that you are interviewing them confidentially, and that their participation is voluntary.

Asking the Questions

You've gotten in. The respondent has asked you to sit down and make yourself comfortable. It may be that the respondent was in the middle of doing something when you arrived and you may need to allow them a few minutes to finish the phone call or send the kids off to do homework. Now, you're ready to begin the interview itself.

— Use questionnaire carefully, but informally.

The questionnaire is your friend. It was developed with a lot of care and thoughtfulness. While you have to be ready to adapt to the needs of the setting, your first instinct should always be to trust the instrument that was designed. But you also need to establish a rapport with the respondent. If you have your face in the instrument and you read the questions, you'll appear unprofessional and disinterested. Even though you may be nervous, you need to recognise that your respondent is most likely even more nervous. If you memorise the first few questions, you can refer to the instrument only occasionally, using eye contact and a confident manner to set the tone for the interview and help the respondent get comfortable.

— Ask questions exactly as written.

Sometimes an interviewer will think that they could improve on the tone of a question by altering a few words to make it simpler or more "friendly." DON'T. You should ask the questions as they are on the instrument. If you had a problem with a question, the time to raise it was during the training and rehearsals, not during the actual interview. It is important that the interview be as standardised as possible across respondents. You may think the change you made was inconsequential when, in fact, it may change the entire meaning of the question or response.

— Follow the order given.

Once you know an interview well, you may see a respondent bring up a topic that you know will come up later in the interview. You may be tempted to jump to that section of the interview while you're on the topic. DON'T. You are more likely to lose your place. You may omit questions that build a foundation for later questions.

— Ask every question.

Sometimes you'll be tempted to omit a question because you thought you already heard what the respondent will say. Don't assume that. For example, let's say you were conducting an interview with college age women about the topic of date rape. In an earlier question, the respondent mentioned that she knew of a woman on her dormitory floor who had been raped on a date within the past year. A few questions later, you are supposed to ask "Do you know of anyone personally who was raped on a date?" You figure you already know that the answer is yes, so you decide to skip the question. Instead, you might say something like "I know you may have already mentioned this, but do you know of anyone personally who was raped on a date?"

— Silent probe.

The most effective way to encourage someone to elaborate is to do nothing at all—just pause and wait. This is referred to as the "silent" probe. It works because the respondent is uncomfortable with pauses or silence. It suggests to the respondent that you are waiting, listening for what they will say next.

— Overt encouragement.

At times, you can encourage the respondent directly. Try to do so in a way that does not imply approval or disapproval of what they said (that could bias their subsequent results). Overt encouragement could be as simple as saying "Uh-huh" or "OK" after the respondent completes a thought.

— Elaboration.

You can encourage more information by asking for

elaboration. For instance, it is appropriate to ask questions like "Would you like to elaborate on that?" or "Is there anything else you would like to add?"

— Ask for clarification.

Sometimes, you can elicit greater detail by asking the respondent to clarify something that was said earlier. You might say, "A minute ago you were talking about the experience you had in high school. Could you tell me more about that?"

— Repetition.

This is the old psychotherapist trick. You say something without really saying anything new. For instance, the respondent just described a traumatic experience they had in childhood. You might say "What I'm hearing you say is that you found that experience very traumatic." Then, you should pause. The respondent is likely to say something like "Well, yes, and it affected the rest of my family as well. In fact, my younger sister..."

Recording the Response

Although we have the capability to record a respondent in audio and/or video, most interview methodologists don't think it's a good idea. Respondents are often uncomfortable when they know their remarks will be recorded word-for-word. They may strain to only say things in a socially acceptable way. Although you would get a more detailed and accurate record, it is likely to be distorted by the very process of obtaining it. This may be more of a problem in some situations than in others. It is increasingly common to be told that your conversation may be recorded during a phone interview. And most focus group methodologies use unobtrusive recording equipment to capture what's being said. But, in general, personal interviews are still best when recorded by the interviewer using pen and paper.

— Record responses immediately.

The interviewer should record responses as they are being stated. This conveys the idea that you are interested enough in what the respondent is saying to write it down. You don't have to write down every single word—you're not taking stenography. But you may want to record certain key phrases or quotes verbatim. You need to develop a system for distinguishing what the respondent says verbatim from what you are characterising.

— Include all probes.

You need to indicate every single probe that you use. Develop a shorthand for different standard probes. Use a clear form for writing them in.

— Use abbreviations where possible.

Abbreviations will help you to capture more of the discussion. Develop a standardised system (e.g., R=respondent; DK=don't know). If you create an abbreviation on the fly, have a way of indicating its origin. For instance, if you decide to abbreviate Spouse with an 'S', you might make a notation in the right margin saying "S=Spouse."

Concluding the Interview

When you've gone through the entire interview, you need to bring the interview to closure. Some important things to remember:

— Thank the respondent.

Don't forget to do this. Even if the respondent was

troublesome or uninformative, it is important for you to be polite and thank them for their time.

— Tell them when you expect to send results.

You owe it to your respondent to show them what you learned. Now, they may not want your entire 300-page dissertation. It's common practice to prepare a short, readable, jargon-free summary of interviews that you can send to the respondents.

— Don't be brusque or hasty.

Allow for a few minutes of winding down conversation. The respondent may want to know a little bit about you or how much you like doing this kind of work. They may be interested in how the results will be used. Use these kinds of interests as a way to wrap up the conversation. As you're putting away your materials and packing up to go, engage the respondent. You don't want the respondent to feel as though you completed the interview and then rushed out on them—they may wonder what they said that was wrong. On the other hand, you have to be careful here. Some respondents may want to keep on talking long after the interview is over. You have to find a way to politely cut off the conversation and make your exit.

— Immediately after leaving—write down any notes about how the interview went.

Sometimes you will have observations about the interview that you didn't want to write down while you were with the respondent. You may have noticed them get upset at a question, or you may have detected hostility in a response. Immediately after the interview you should go over your notes and make any other comments and observations—but be sure to distinguish these from the notes made during the interview.

8

Evaluation Research

Evaluation can be a threatening activity. Many groups and organisations struggle with how to build a good evaluation capability into their everyday activities and procedures. This is essentially an organisational culture issue. Here we consider some of the issues a group or organisation needs to address in order to develop an evaluation culture that works in their context. Evaluation is a methodological area that is closely related to, but distinguishable from more traditional social research.

Evaluation utilises many of the same methodologies used in traditional social research, but because evaluation takes place within a political and organisational context, it requires group skills, management ability, political dexterity, sensitivity to multiple stakeholders and other skills that social research in general does not rely on as much.

DEFINITIONS OF EVALUATION

Probably the most frequently given definition is:

> Evaluation is the systematic assessment of the worth or merit of some object

This definition is hardly perfect. There are many types of evaluations that do not necessarily result in an assessment of worth or merit—descriptive studies, implementation analyses, and formative evaluations, to name a few. Better perhaps is a definition that emphasizes the information-processing and feedback functions of evaluation. For instance, one might say:

> Evaluation is the systematic acquisition and assessment of information to provide useful feedback about some object

Both definitions agree that evaluation is a systematic endeavour and both use the deliberately ambiguous term 'object' which could refer to a programme, policy, technology, person, need, activity, and so on. The latter definition emphasises acquiring and assessing information rather than assessing worth or merit because all evaluation work involves collecting and sifting through data, making judgements about the validity of the information and of inferences we derive from it, whether or not an assessment of worth or merit results.

GOALS OF EVALUATION

The generic goal of most evaluations is to provide "useful feedback" to a variety of audiences including sponsors, donors, client-groups, administrators, staff, and other relevant constituencies. Most often, feedback is perceived as "useful" if it aids in decision-making.

But the relationship between an evaluation and its impact is not a simple one—studies that seem critical sometimes fail to influence short-term decisions, and studies that initially seem to have no influence can have a delayed impact when more congenial conditions arise. Despite this, there is broad consensus that the major goal of evaluation should be to influence decision-making or policy formulation through the provision of empirically-driven feedback.

GROUPS OF EVALUATION STRATEGIES

'Evaluation strategies' means broad, overarching perspectives on evaluation. They encompass the most general groups or "camps" of evaluators; although, at its best, evaluation work borrows eclectically from the perspectives of all these camps. Four major groups of evaluation strategies are discussed here.

Scientific-experimental models are probably the most historically dominant evaluation strategies. Taking their values and methods from the sciences—especially the social sciences—they prioritize on the desirability of impartiality, accuracy, objectivity and the validity of the information generated. Included under scientific-experimental models would be: the tradition of experimental and quasi-experimental designs; objectives-based research that comes from education; econometrically-oriented perspectives including cost-effectiveness and cost-benefit analysis; and the recent articulation of theory-driven evaluation.

The second class of strategies are management-oriented systems models. Two of the most common of these are PERT, the Programme Evaluation and Review Technique, and CPM, the Critical Path Method. Both have been widely used in business and government in America. It would also be legitimate to include the Logical Framework or "Logframe" model developed at U.S. Agency for International Development and general systems theory and operations research approaches in this category.

The third class of strategies are the qualitative/anthropological models. They emphasise the importance of observation, the need to retain the phenomenological quality of the evaluation context, and the value of subjective human interpretation in the evaluation process. Included in this category are the approaches known in evaluation as naturalistic or 'Fourth Generation' evaluation; the various qualitative schools; critical theory and art criticism approaches; and, the 'grounded theory' approach of Glaser and Strauss among others.

Finally, a fourth class of strategies is termed participant-oriented models. As the term suggests, they emphasise the central importance of the evaluation participants, especially clients and users of the programme or technology. Client-centred and stakeholder approaches are examples of participant-oriented models, as are consumer-oriented evaluation systems. With all of these strategies to choose from, how to decide? Debates that rage within the evaluation profession—and they do rage—are generally battles between these different strategists, with each claiming the superiority of their position.

In reality, most good evaluators are familiar with all four categories and borrow from each as the need arises. There is no inherent incompatibility between these broad strategies—each of them brings something valuable to the evaluation table. In fact, in recent years attention has increasingly turned to how one might integrate results from evaluations that use different strategies, carried out from different perspectives, and using different methods. Clearly, there are no simple answers here. The problems are complex and the methodologies needed will and should be varied.

FORMATIVE AND SUMMATIVE EVALUATION

There are many different types of evaluations depending on the object being evaluated and the purpose of the evaluation. Perhaps the most important basic distinction in evaluation types is that between formative and summative evaluation. Formative evaluations strengthen or improve the object being evaluated—they help form it by examining the delivery of the programme or technology, the quality of its implementation, and the assessment of the organisational context, personnel, procedures, inputs, and so on.

Summative evaluations, in contrast, examine the effects or outcomes of some object—they summarise it by describing what happens subsequent to delivery of the programme or technology; assessing whether the object can be said to have caused the outcome; determining the overall impact of the causal factor beyond only the immediate target outcomes; and, estimating the relative costs associated with the object.

Formative evaluation includes several evaluation types:

— Needs assessment determines who needs the programme, how great the need is, and what might work to meet the need.

— Evaluability assessment determines whether an evaluation is feasible and how stakeholders can help shape its usefulness.

— Structured conceptualisation helps stakeholders define the programme or technology, the target population, and the possible outcomes.

— Implementation evaluation monitors the fidelity of the programme or technology delivery.

— Process evaluation investigates the process of delivering the programme or technology, including alternative delivery procedures.

Summative evaluation can also be subdivided:

— Outcome evaluations investigate whether the programme or technology caused demonstrable effects on specifically defined target outcomes.

— Impact evaluation is broader and assesses the overall or net effects—intended or unintended—of the programme or technology as a whole.

— Cost-effectiveness and cost-benefit analysis address questions of efficiency by standardising outcomes in terms of their dollar costs and values.

— Secondary analysis reexamines existing data to address new questions or use methods not previously employed.

— Meta-analysis integrates the outcome estimates from multiple studies to arrive at an overall or summary judgement on an evaluation question.

QUESTIONS AND METHODS OF EVALUATION

Evaluators ask many different kinds of questions and use a variety of methods to address them. These are considered within the framework of formative and summative evaluation as presented above.

In formative research the major questions and methodologies are:

— What is the definition and scope of the problem or issue, or what's the question?

Formulating and conceptualising methods might be used including brainstorming, focus groups, nominal group techniques, Delphi methods, brainwriting, stakeholder analysis, synectics, lateral thinking, input-output analysis, and concept mapping.

— Where is the problem and how big or serious is it?

The most common method used here is "needs assessment" which can include: analysis of existing data sources, and the use of sample surveys, interviews of constituent populations, qualitative research, expert testimony, and focus groups.

— How should the programme or technology be delivered to address the problem?

Some of the methods already listed apply here, as do detailing methodologies like simulation techniques, or multivariate methods like multiattribute utility theory or exploratory causal modelling; decision-making methods; and project planning and implementation methods like flow charting, PERT/CPM, and project scheduling.

— How well is the programme or technology delivered?

Qualitative and quantitative monitoring techniques, the use of management information systems, and implementation assessment would be appropriate methodologies here.

The questions and methods addressed under summative evaluation include:

— What type of evaluation is feasible?

Evaluability assessment can be used here, as well as standard approaches for selecting an appropriate evaluation design.

— What was the effectiveness of the programme or technology?

One would choose from observational and correlational methods for demonstrating whether desired effects occurred, and quasi-experimental and experimental designs for determining whether observed effects can reasonably be attributed to the intervention and not to other sources.

— What is the net impact of the programme?

Econometric methods for assessing cost effectiveness and cost/benefits would apply here, along with qualitative methods that enable us to summarise the full range of intended and unintended impacts.

Clearly, this introduction is not meant to be exhaustive. Each of these methods, and the many not mentioned, are supported by an extensive methodological research literature. This is a formidable set of tools. But the need to improve, update and adapt these methods to changing circumstances means that methodological research and development needs to have a major place in evaluation work.

PLANNING-EVALUATION CYCLE

Often, evaluation is construed as part of a larger managerial or administrative process. Sometimes this is referred to as the planning-evaluation cycle. The distinctions between planning and evaluation are not always clear; this cycle is described in many different ways with various phases claimed by both planners and evaluators. Usually, the first stage of such a cycle—the planning phase—is designed to elaborate a set of potential actions, programmes, or technologies, and select the best for implementation.

Depending on the organisation and the problem being addressed, a planning process could involve any or all of these stages: the formulation of the problem, issue, or concern; the broad conceptualisation of the major alternatives that might be considered; the detailing of these alternatives and their potential implications; the evaluation of the alternatives and the selection of the best one; and the implementation of the selected alternative. Although these stages are traditionally considered planning, there is a lot of evaluation work involved.

Evaluators are trained in needs assessment, they use methodologies—like the concept mapping one presented later—that help in conceptualisation and detailing, and they have the skills to help assess alternatives and make a choice of the best one. The evaluation phase also involves a sequence of stages that typically includes: the formulation of the major objectives, goals, and hypotheses of the programme or technology; the conceptualisation and operationalisation of the major components of the evaluation—the programme, participants, setting, and measures; the design of the evaluation, detailing how these components will be coordinated; the analysis of the information, both qualitative and quantitative; and the utilisation of the evaluation results.

EVALUATION CULTURE

An evaluation culture will embrace an action-oriented perspective that actively seeks solutions to problems, trying out tentative ones, weighing the results and consequences of actions, all within an endless cycle of supposition-action-evidence-revision that characterises good science and good management. In this activist evaluation culture, we will encourage innovative approaches at all levels. But well-intentioned activism by itself is not enough, and may at times be risky, dangerous, and lead to detrimental consequences.

In an evaluation culture, we won't act for action's sake—we'll always attempt to assess the effects of our actions. This evaluation culture will be an accessible, teaching-oriented one that emphasises the unity of formal evaluation and everyday thought. Most of our evaluations will be simple, informal, efficient, practical, low-cost and easily carried out and understood by nontechnicians. Evaluations won't just be delegated to one person or department—we will encourage everyone in our organisations to become involved in evaluating what they and their organisations do.

Where technical expertise is needed we will encourage the experts to also educate us about the technical side of what they do, demanding that they try to find ways to explain their techniques and methods adequately for nontechnicians. We will devote considerable resources to teaching others about evaluation principles. Our evaluation culture will be diverse, inclusive, participatory, responsive and fundamentally non-hierarchical. World problems cannot be solved by simple "silver bullet" solutions. There is growing recognition in many arenas that our most fundamental problems are systemic, interconnected, and inextricably linked to social and economic issues and factors. Solutions will involve husbanding the resources, talents and insights of a wide range of people.

The formulation of problems and potential solutions needs to involve a broad range of constituencies. More than just "research" skills will be needed. Especially important will be skills in negotiation and consensus-building processes. Evaluators are familiar with arguments for greater diversity and inclusiveness—we've been talking about stakeholder, participative, multiple-constituency research for nearly two decades. Our evaluation culture will be a humble, self-critical one. We will openly acknowledge our limitations and recognise that what we learn from a single evaluation study, however well designed, will almost always be equivocal and tentative.

In this regard, we believe we too often undervalue cowardice in research. We find it wholly appropriate that evaluators resist being drawn into making decisions for others, although certainly the results of our work should help inform the decision makers. A cowardly approach saves the evaluator from being drawn into the political context, helping assure the impartiality needed for objective assessment, and it protects the evaluator from taking responsibility for making decisions that should be left to those who have been duly-authorised—and who have to live with the consequences.

Most programme decisions, especially decisions about whether to continue a programme or close it down, must include more input than an evaluation alone can ever provide. While evaluators can help to elucidate what has happened in the past or might happen under certain circumstances, it is the responsibility of the organisation and society as a whole to determine what ought to happen. Our evaluation culture will need to be an interdisciplinary one, doing more than just grafting one discipline onto another through constructing multi-discipline research teams. We'll need such teams, of course, but we mean to imply something deeper, more personally internalised—we need to move toward being nondisciplinary, consciously putting aside the blinders of our respective specialties in an attempt to foster a more whole view of the phenomena we study.

As we consider the programmes we are evaluating, we each should be able to speculate about a broad range of implementation factors or potential consequences. We should be able to anticipate some of the organisational and systems-related features of these programmes, the economic factors that might enhance or reduce implementation, their social and psychological dimensions, and especially whether the ultimate utilisers can understand or know how to utilise and be willing to utilise the the results of our evaluation work. We should also be able to anticipate a broad spectrum of potential consequences—system-related, production-related, economic, nutritional, social, environmental. This evaluation culture will also be an honest, truth-seeking one that stresses accountability and scientific credibility.

In many quarters in contemporary society, it appears that many people have given up on the ideas of truth and validity. Our evaluation culture needs to hold to the goal of getting at the truth while at the same time honestly acknowledging the revisability of all scientific knowledge. We need to be critical of those who have given up on the goal of "getting it right" about reality, especially those among the humanities and social sciences who argue that truth is entirely relative to the knower, objectivity an impossibility, and reality nothing more than a construction or illusion that cannot be examined publicly. For them, the goal of seeking the truth is inappropriate and unacceptable, and science a tool of oppression rather than a road to greater enlightenment.

Philosophers have, of course, debated such issues for thousands of years and will undoubtedly do so for thousands more. We in the evaluation culture need to check in on their thinking from time to time, but until they settle these debates, we need to hold steadfastly to the goal of getting at the truth—the goal of getting it right about reality. Our evaluation culture will be prospective and forward-looking, anticipating where evaluation feedback will be needed rather than just reacting to situations as they arise. We will construct simple, low-cost evaluation and monitoring information systems when we first initiate a new programme or technology—we cannot wait until a programme is complete or a technology is in the field before we turn our attention to its evaluation.

Finally, the evaluation culture we envision is one that will emphasise fair, open, ethical and democratic processes. We should move away from private ownership of and exclusive access to data. The data from all of our evaluations needs to be accessible to all interested groups allowing more extensive independent secondary analyses and opportunities for replication or refutation of original results. We should encourage open commentary and debate regarding the results of specific evaluations. Especially when there are multiple parties who have a stake in such results, it is important for our reporting procedures to include formal opportunities for competitive review and response.

9

Case Study as a Research Method

The case study is one of several ways of doing social science research. Other ways include experiments, surveys, multiple histories, and analysis of archival information. Rather than using large samples and following a rigid protocol to examine a limited number of variables, case study methods involve an in-depth, longitudinal examination of a single instance or event: a case. They provide a systematic way of looking at events, collecting data, analysing information, and reporting the results.

As a result the researcher may gain a sharpened understanding of why the instance happened as it did, and what might become important to look at more extensively in future research. Case studies lend themselves to both generating and testing hypotheses. Another suggestion is that case study should be defined as a research strategy, an empirical inquiry that investigates a phenomenon within its real-life context.

Case study research means single and multiple case studies, can include quantitative evidence, relies on multiple sources of evidence and benefits from the prior development of theoretical propositions. Case studies should not be confused with qualitative research and they can be based on any mix of quantitative and qualitative evidence. Single-subject research provides the statistical framework for making inferences from quantitative case-study data.

CASE SELECTION

When selecting a case for a case study, researchers often use information-oriented sampling, as opposed to random sampling. This is because the typical or average case is often not the richest in information. Extreme or atypical cases reveal more information because they activate more basic mechanisms and more actors in the situation studied.

In addition, from both an understanding-oriented and an action-oriented perspective, it is often more important to clarify the deeper causes behind a given problem and its consequences than to describe the symptoms of the problem and how frequently they occur. Random samples emphasizing representativeness will seldom be able to produce this kind of insight; it is more appropriate to select some few cases chosen for their validity.

Three types of information-oriented cases may be distinguished:

— Extreme or deviant cases.

— Critical cases.

— Paradigmatic cases.

Extreme Case

The extreme case can be well-suited for getting a point across in an especially dramatic way, which often occurs for well-known case studies such as in Freud's 'Wolf-Man.'

Critical Case

A critical case can be defined as having strategic

importance in relation to the general problem. For example, an occupational medicine clinic wanted to investigate whether people working with organic solvents suffered brain damage. Instead of choosing a representative sample among all those enterprises in the clinic's area that used organic solvents, the clinic strategically located a single workplace where all safety regulations on cleanliness, air quality, and the like, had been fulfilled. This model enterprise became a critical case: if brain damage related to organic solvents could be found at this particular facility, then it was likely that the same problem would exist at other enterprises which were less careful with safety regulations for organic solvents.

Via this type of strategic sampling, one can save both time and money in researching a given problem. Another example of critical case sampling is the strategic selection of lead and feather for the test of whether different objects fall with equal velocity. The selection of materials provided the possibility to formulate a generalisation characteristic of critical cases, a generalisation of the sort, 'If it is valid for this case, it is valid for all cases.' In its negative form, the generalisation would be, 'If it is not valid for this case, then it is not valid for any cases.'

Paradigmatic Case

A Paradigmatic case may be defined as an exemplar or prototype. Thomas Kuhn has shown that the basic skills, or background practices, of natural scientists are organised in terms of 'exemplars' or 'paradigms' the role of which in the scientific process can be analysed. Similarly, scholars like Clifford Geertz and Michel Foucault have often organised their research around specific cultural paradigms: a paradigm for Geertz lay for instance in the 'deep play' of the Balinese cockfight, while for Foucault, European prisons and the 'Panopticon' are examples.

Both instances are examples of paradigmatic cases, that is, cases that highlight more general characteristics of the societies or issues in question. Kuhn has shown that scientific paradigms cannot be expressed as rules or theories. There exists no predictive theory for how predictive theory comes about. A scientific activity is acknowledged or rejected as good science by how close it is to one or more exemplars; that is, practical prototypes of good scientific work. A paradigmatic case of how scientists do science is precisely such a prototype. It operates as a reference point and may function as a focus for the founding of schools of thought.

GENERALISING FROM CASE STUDIES

The case study is effective for generalising using the type of test that Karl Popper called falsification, which forms part of critical reflexivity. Falsification is one of the most rigorous tests to which a scientific proposition can be subjected: if just one observation does not fit with the proposition it is considered not valid generally and must therefore be either revised or rejected. Popper himself used the now famous example of, "All swans are white," and proposed that just one observation of a single black swan would falsify this proposition and in this way have general significance and stimulate further investigations and theory-building.

The case study is well suited for identifying "black swans" because of its in-depth approach: what appears to be "white" often turns out on closer examination to be "black." For instance, Galileo's rejection of Aristotle's law of gravity was based on a case study selected by information-oriented sampling and not random sampling. The rejection consisted primarily of a conceptual experiment and later on of a practical one. These experiments, with the benefit of hindsight, are self-evident.

Nevertheless, Aristotle's incorrect view of gravity dominated scientific inquiry for nearly two thousand years before it was falsified. In his experimental thinking, Galileo reasoned as follows: if two objects with the same weight are released from the same height at the same time, they will hit the ground simultaneously, having fallen at the same speed. If the two objects are then stuck together into one, this object will have double the weight and will according to the Aristotelian view therefore fall faster than the two individual objects. This conclusion seemed contradictory to Galileo.

The only way to avoid the contradiction was to eliminate weight as a determinant factor for acceleration in free fall. Galileo's experimentalism did not involve a large random sample of trials of objects falling from a wide range of randomly selected heights under varying wind conditions, and so on. Rather, it was a matter of a single experiment, that is, a case study. Galileo's view continued to be subjected to doubt, however, and the Aristotelian view was not finally rejected until half a century later, with the invention of the air pump.

The air pump made it possible to conduct the ultimate experiment, known by every pupil, whereby a coin or a piece of lead inside a vacuum tube falls with the same speed as a feather. After this experiment, Aristotle's view could be maintained no longer. What is especially worth noting, however, is that the matter was settled by an individual case due to the clever choice of the extremes of metal and feather. One might call it a critical case, for if Galileo's thesis held for these materials, it could be expected to be valid for all or a large range of materials. Random and large samples were at no time part of the picture. However it was Galileo's view that was the subject of doubt as it was not reasonable enough to be Aristotelian view. By selecting cases strategically in this manner one may arrive at case studies that allow generalisation.

ORIGIN OF THE CASE STUDY METHOD

As a distinct approach to research, use of the case study originated only in the early 20th century. The Oxford English Dictionary traces the phrase case study or case-study back as far as 1934, after the establishment of the concept of a case history in medicine. The use of case studies for the creation of new theory in social sciences has been further developed by the sociologists Barney Glaser and Anselm Strauss who presented their research method, Grounded theory, in 1967.

The popularity of case studies in testing hypotheses has developed only in recent decades. One of the areas in which case studies have been gaining popularity is education and in particular educational evaluation. Case studies have also been used as a teaching method and as part of professional development, especially in business and legal education. The problem-based learning (PBL) movement is such an example. When used in education and professional development, case studies are often referred to as critical incidents.

CASE STUDY RESEARCH

Case study research excels at bringing us to an understanding of a complex issue or object and can extend experience or add strength to what is already known through previous research. Case studies emphasise detailed contextual analysis of a limited number of events or conditions and their relationships. Researchers have used the case study research method for many years across a variety of disciplines.

Social scientists, in particular, have made wide use of this qualitative research method to examine contemporary real-life situations and provide the basis for the application of ideas and extension of methods. Researcher Robert K. Yin defines the case study research method as an empirical inquiry that investigates a contemporary phenomenon within its real-life context; when the boundaries between phenomenon and context are not clearly evident; and in which multiple sources of evidence are used. Critics of the case study method believe that the study of a small number of cases can offer no grounds for establishing reliability or generality of findings. Others feel that the intense exposure to study of the case biases the findings. Some dismiss case study research as useful only as an exploratory tool. Yet researchers continue to use the case study research method with success in carefully planned and crafted studies of real-life situations, issues, and problems.

Reports on case studies from many disciplines are widely available in the literature. This paper explains how to use the case study method and then applies the method to an example case study project designed to examine how one set of users, non-profit organisations, make use of an electronic community network. The study examines the issue of whether or not the electronic community network is beneficial in some way to non-profit organisations and what those benefits might be. Many well-known case study researchers such as Robert E. Stake, Helen Simons, and Robert K. Yin have written about case study research and suggested techniques for organising and conducting the research successfully. This introduction to case study research draws upon their work and proposes six steps that should be used:

— Determine and define the research questions.

— Select the cases and determine data gathering and analysis techniques.

— Prepare to collect the data.
— Collect data in the field.
— Evaluate and analyse the data.
— Prepare the report.

Determine and Define the Research Questions

The first step in case study research is to establish a firm research focus to which the researcher can refer over the course of study of a complex phenomenon or object. The researcher establishes the focus of the study by forming questions about the situation or problem to be studied and determining a purpose for the study. The research object in a case study is often a programme, an entity, a person, or a group of people. Each object is likely to be intricately connected to political, social, historical, and personal issues, providing wide ranging possibilities for questions and adding complexity to the case study.

The researcher investigates the object of the case study in depth using a variety of data gathering methods to produce evidence that leads to understanding of the case and answers the research questions. Case study research generally answers one or more questions which begin with "how" or "why." The questions are targeted to a limited number of events or conditions and their inter-relationships.

To assist in targeting and formulating the questions, researchers conduct a literature review. This review establishes what research has been previously conducted and leads to refined, insightful questions about the problem. Careful definition of the questions at the start pinpoints where to look for evidence and helps determine the methods of analysis to be used in the study. The literature review, definition of the purpose of the case study, and early determination of the potential audience for the final report guide how the study will be designed, conducted, and publicly reported.

Select the Cases and Determine Data Gathering and Analysis Techniques

During the design phase of case study research, the researcher determines what approaches to use in selecting single or multiple real-life cases to examine in depth and which instruments and data gathering approaches to use. When using multiple cases, each case is treated as a single case. Each case's conclusions can then be used as information contributing to the whole study, but each case remains a single case. Exemplary case studies carefully select cases and carefully examine the choices available from among many research tools available in order to increase the validity of the study. Careful discrimination at the point of selection also helps erect boundaries around the case.

The researcher must determine whether to study cases which are unique in some way or cases which are considered typical and may also select cases to represent a variety of geographic regions, a variety of size parameters, or other parameters. A useful step in the selection process is to repeatedly refer back to the purpose of the study in order to focus attention on where to look for cases and evidence that will satisfy the purpose of the study and answer the research questions posed.

Selecting multiple or single cases is a key element, but a case study can include more than one unit of embedded analysis. For example, a case study may involve study of a single industry and a firm participating in that industry. This type of case study involves two levels of analysis and increases the complexity and amount of data to be gathered and analysed. A key strength of the case study method involves using multiple sources and techniques in the data gathering process. The researcher determines in advance what evidence to gather and what analysis techniques to use with the data to answer the research questions.

Data gathered is normally largely qualitative, but it may also be quantitative. Tools to collect data can include surveys, interviews, documentation review, observation, and even the collection of physical artifacts. The researcher must use the designated data gathering tools systematically and properly in collecting the evidence. Throughout the design phase, researchers must ensure that the study is well constructed to ensure construct validity, internal validity, external validity, and reliability. Construct validity requires the researcher to use the correct measures for the concepts being studied.

Internal validity demonstrates that certain conditions lead to other conditions and requires the use of multiple pieces of evidence from multiple sources to uncover convergent lines of inquiry. The researcher strives to establish a chain of evidence forward and backward. External validity reflects whether or not findings are generalisable beyond the immediate case or cases; the more variations in places, people, and procedures a case study can withstand and still yield the same findings, the more external validity. Techniques such as cross-case examination and within-case examination along with literature review helps ensure external validity. Reliability refers to the stability, accuracy, and precision of measurement. Exemplary case study design ensures that the procedures used are well documented and can be repeated with the same results over and over again.

Prepare to Collect the Data

Because case study research generates a large amount of

data from multiple sources, systematic organisation of the data is important to prevent the researcher from becoming overwhelmed by the amount of data and to prevent the researcher from losing sight of the original research purpose and questions. Advance preparation assists in handling large amounts of data in a documented and systematic fashion. Researchers prepare databases to assist with categorising, sorting, storing, and retrieving data for analysis.

Exemplary case studies prepare good training programmes for investigators, establish clear protocols and procedures in advance of investigator field work, and conduct a pilot study in advance of moving into the field in order to remove obvious barriers and problems. The investigator training programme covers the basic concepts of the study, terminology, processes, and methods, and teaches investigators how to properly apply the techniques being used in the study. The programme also trains investigators to understand how the gathering of data using multiple techniques strengthens the study by providing opportunities for triangulation during the analysis phase of the study.

The programme covers protocols for case study research, including time deadlines, formats for narrative reporting and field notes, guidelines for collection of documents, and guidelines for field procedures to be used. Investigators need to be good listeners who can hear exactly the words being used by those interviewed. Qualifications for investigators also include being able to ask good questions and interpret answers. Good investigators review documents looking for facts, but also read between the lines and pursue collaborative evidence elsewhere when that seems appropriate.

Investigators need to be flexible in real-life situations and not feel threatened by unexpected change, missed appointments, or lack of office space. Investigators need to understand the purpose of the study and grasp the issues and must be open to contrary findings. Investigators must also be aware that they are going into the world of real human beings who may be threatened or unsure of what the case study will bring.

After investigators are trained, the final advance preparation step is to select a pilot site and conduct a pilot test using each data gathering method so that problematic areas can be uncovered and corrected. Researchers need to anticipate key problems and events, identify key people, prepare letters of introduction, establish rules for confidentiality, and actively seek opportunities to revisit and revise the research design in order to address and add to the original set of research questions.

Collect Data in the Field

The researcher must collect and store multiple sources of evidence comprehensively and systematically, in formats that can be referenced and sorted so that converging lines of inquiry and patterns can be uncovered. Researchers carefully observe the object of the case study and identify causal factors associated with the observed phenomenon. Renegotiation of arrangements with the objects of the study or addition of questions to interviews may be necessary as the study progresses.

Case study research is flexible, but when changes are made, they are documented systematically. Exemplary case studies use field notes and databases to categorise and reference data so that it is readily available for subsequent reinterpretation. Field notes record feelings and intuitive hunches, pose questions, and document the work in progress. They record testimonies, stories, and illustrations which can be used in later reports. They may warn of impending bias because of the detailed exposure of the client to special attention, or give an early signal that a pattern is emerging.

They assist in determining whether or not the inquiry needs to be reformulated or redefined based on what is being observed. Field notes should be kept separate from the data being collected and stored for analysis. Maintaining the relationship between the issue and the evidence is mandatory. The researcher may enter some data into a database and physically store other data, but the researcher documents, classifies, and cross-references all evidence so that it can be efficiently recalled for sorting and examination over the course of the study.

Data Analysis

The researcher examines raw data using many interpretations in order to find linkages between the research object and the outcomes with reference to the original research questions. Throughout the evaluation and analysis process, the researcher remains open to new opportunities and insights. The case study method, with its use of multiple data collection methods and analysis techniques, provides researchers with opportunities to triangulate data in order to strengthen the research findings and conclusions.

The tactics used in analysis force researchers to move beyond initial impressions to improve the likelihood of accurate and reliable findings. Exemplary case studies will deliberately sort the data in many different ways to expose or create new insights and will deliberately look for conflicting data to disconfirm the analysis. Researchers categorise, tabulate, and recombine data to address the initial propositions or purpose of the study, and conduct cross-checks of facts and discrepancies in accounts. Focused, short, repeat interviews may be necessary to gather additional data to verify key observations or check a fact.

Specific techniques include placing information into arrays, creating matrices of categories, creating flow charts or other displays, and tabulating frequency of events. Researchers use the quantitative data that has been collected to corroborate and support the qualitative data which is most useful for understanding the rationale or theory underlying relationships. Another technique is to use multiple investigators to gain the advantage provided when a variety of perspectives and insights examine the data and the patterns.

When the multiple observations converge, confidence in the findings increases. Conflicting perceptions, on the other hand, cause the researchers to pry more deeply. Another technique, the cross-case search for patterns, keeps investigators from reaching premature conclusions by requiring that investigators look at the data in many different ways. Cross-case analysis divides the data by type across all cases investigated.

One researcher then examines the data of that type thoroughly. When a pattern from one data type is corroborated by the evidence from another, the finding is stronger. When evidence conflicts, deeper probing of the differences is necessary to identify the cause or source of conflict. In all cases, the researcher treats the evidence fairly to produce analytic conclusions answering the original "how" and "why" research questions.

Prepare the Report

Exemplary case studies report the data in a way that transforms a complex issue into one that can be understood, allowing the reader to question and examine the study and reach an understanding independent of the researcher. The goal of the written report is to portray a complex problem in a way that conveys a vicarious experience to the reader.

Case studies present data in very publicly accessible ways and may lead the reader to apply the experience in his or her own real-life situation. Researchers pay particular attention to displaying sufficient evidence to gain the reader's confidence that all avenues have been explored, clearly communicating the boundaries of the case, and giving special attention to conflicting propositions. Techniques for composing the report can include handling each case as a separate chapter or treating the case as a chronological recounting. Some researchers report the case study as a story.

During the report preparation process, researchers critically examine the document looking for ways the report is incomplete. The researcher uses representative audience groups to review and comment on the draft document. Based on the comments, the researcher rewrites and makes revisions. Some case study researchers suggest that the document review audience include a journalist and some suggest that the documents should be reviewed by the participants in the study.

ELECTRONIC COMMUNITY NETWORK

By way of example, we apply these six steps to an example study of multiple participants in an electronic community network. All participants are non-profit organisations which have chosen an electronic community network on the World Wide Web as a method of delivering information to the public. The case study method is applicable to this set of users because it can be used to examine the issue of whether or not the electronic community network is beneficial in some way to the organisation and what those benefits might be.

Determine and Define the Research Questions

In general, electronic community networks have three

distinct types of users, each one a good candidate for case study research. The three groups of users include people around the world who use the electronic community network, the non-profit organisations using the electronic community network to provide information to potential users of their services, and the "community" that forms as the result of interacting with other participants on the electronic community network. In this case, the researcher is primarily interested in determining whether or not the electronic community network is beneficial in some way to non-profit organisation participants.

Determine Data Gathering and Analysis Techniques

Many communities have constructed electronic community networks on the World Wide Web. At the outset of the design phase, the researcher determines that only one of these networks will be studied and further sets the study boundaries to include only some of the non-profit organisations represented on that one network. The researcher contacts the Board of Directors of the community network, who are open to the idea of the case study.

The researcher also gathers computer generated log data from the network and, using this data, determines that an in-depth study of representative organisations from four categories—health care, environmental, education, and religious—is feasible. The investigator applies additional selection criteria so that an urban-based and a rural-based non-profit are represented in the study in order to examine whether urban non-profits perceive more benefits from community networks than rural organisations.

The researcher considers multiple sources of data for this study and selects document examination, the gathering and study of organisational documents such as administrative reports, agendas, letters, minutes, and news clippings for each of the organisations. In this case, the investigator decides to also conduct open-ended interviews with key members of each organisation using a check-list to guide interviewers during the interview process so that uniformity and consistency can be assured in the data, which could include facts, opinions, and unexpected insights.

In this case study, the researcher cannot employ direct observation as a tool because some of the organisations involved have no office and meet infrequently to conduct business directly related to the electronic community network. The researcher instead decides to survey all Board members of the selected organisations using a questionnaire as a third data gathering tool. Within-case and cross-case analysis of data are selected as analysis techniques.

Prepare to Collect the Data

The researcher prepares to collect data by first contacting each organisation to be studied to gain their cooperation, explain the purpose of the study, and assemble key contact information. Since data to be collected and examined includes organisational documents, the researcher states his intent to request copies of these documents, and plans for storage, classification, and retrieval of these items, as well as the interview and survey data. The researcher develops a formal investigator training programme to include seminar topics on non-profit organisations and their structures in each of the four categories selected for this study.

The training programme also includes practice sessions in conducting open-ended interviews and documenting sources, suggested field notes formats, and a detailed explanation of the purpose of the case study.

The researcher selects a fifth case as a pilot case, and the investigators apply the data gathering tools to the pilot case to determine whether the planned timeline is feasible and whether or not the interview and survey questions are appropriate and effective. Based on the results of the pilot, the researcher makes adjustments and assigns investigators particular cases which become their area of expertise in the evaluation and analysis of the data.

Collect Data in the Field

Investigators first arrange to visit with the Board of Directors of each non-profit organisation as a group and ask for copies of the organisation's mission, news clippings, brochures, and any other written material describing the organisation and its purpose. The investigator reviews the purpose of the study with the entire Board, schedules individual interview times with as many Board members as can cooperate, confirms key contact data, and requests that all Board members respond to the written survey which will be mailed later.

Investigators take written notes during the interview and record field notes after the interview is completed. The interviews, although open-ended, are structured around the research questions defined at the start of the case study.

— *Research Question*: Why do non-profit organisation participants use the network?

— *Interview Questions*: How did the organisation make the decision to place data on the World Wide Web community network? What need was the organisation hoping to fulfil?

— *Research Question*: How do non-profit organisation participants determine what to place on the electronic community network?

— *Interview Questions*: What process was used to select the information that would be used on the network? How is the information kept up to date?
— *Research Question*: Do the non-profit organisation participants believe the community network serves a useful purpose in furthering their mission? How?
— *Interview Questions*: How does the organisation know if the electronic community network is beneficial to the organisation? How does the electronic community network further the mission of the organisation? What systematic tracking mechanisms exist to determine how many or what types of users are accessing the organisation information?

The investigator's field notes record impressions and questions that might assist with the interpretation of the interview data. The investigator makes note of stories told during open-ended interviews and flags them for potential use in the final report. Data is entered into the database. The researcher mails written surveys to all Board members with a requested return date and a stamped return envelope. Once the surveys are returned, the researcher codes and enters the data into the database so that it can be used independently as well as integrated when the case study progresses to the point of cross-case examination of data for all four cases.

Evaluate and Analyse the Data

Within-case analysis is the first analysis technique used with each non-profit organisation under study. The assigned investigator studies each organisation's written documentation and survey response data as a separate case to identify unique patterns within the data for that single organisation. Individual investigators prepare detailed case study write-ups for each organisation, categorising interview questions and answers and examining the data for within-group similarities and differences. Cross-case analysis follows. Investigators examine pairs of cases, categorising the similarities and differences in each pair. Investigators then examine similar pairs for differences, and dissimilar pairs for similarities. As patterns begin to emerge, certain evidence may stand out as being in conflict with the patterns.

Prepare the Report

The outline of the report includes thanking all of the participants, stating the problem, listing the research questions, describing the methods used to conduct the research and any potential flaws in the method used, explaining the data gathering and analysis techniques used, and concluding with the answers to the questions and suggestions for further research. Key features of the report include a retelling of specific stories related to the successes or disappointments experienced by the organisations that were conveyed during data collection, and answers or comments illuminating issues directly related to the research questions.

The researcher develops each issue using quotations or other details from the data collected, and points out the triangulation of data where applicable. The report also includes confirming and conflicting findings from literature reviews. The report conclusion makes assertions and suggestions for further research activity, so that another researcher may apply these techniques to another electronic community network and its participants to determine whether similar findings are identifiable in other communities. Final report distribution includes all participants.

10

Action Research Method

Action research is a reflective process of progressive problem solving led by individuals working with others in teams or as part of a "community of practice" to improve the way they address issues and solve problems. Action research can also be undertaken by larger organisations or institutions, assisted or guided by professional researchers, with the aim of improving their strategies, practices, and knowledge of the environments within which they practice.

Kurt Lewin, then a professor at MIT, first coined the term "action research" in about 1944, and it appears in his 1946 paper "Action Research and Minority Problems". In that paper, he described action research as "a comparative research on the conditions and effects of various forms of social action and research leading to social action" that uses "a spiral of steps, each of which is composed of a circle of planning, action, and fact-finding about the result of the action".

Action research challenges traditional social science, by moving beyond reflective knowledge created by outside experts sampling variables to an active moment-to-moment theorising, data collecting, and inquiring occurring in the midst of emergent structure. "Knowledge is always gained through action and for action. From this starting point, to question the validity of social knowledge is to question, not how to develop a reflective science about action, but how to develop genuinely well-informed action—how to conduct an action science".

Action research is known by many other names, including participatory research, collaborative inquiry, emancipatory research, action learning, and contextural action research, but all are variations on a theme. Put simply, action research is "learning by doing"—a group of people identify a problem, do something to resolve it, see how successful their efforts were, and if not satisfied, try again. While this is the essence of the approach, there are other key attributes of action research that differentiate it from common problem-solving activities that we all engage in every day. A more succinct definition is:

> "Action research...aims to contribute both to the practical concerns of people in an immediate problematic situation and to further the goals of social science simultaneously. Thus, there is a dual commitment in action research to study a system and concurrently to collaborate with members of the system in changing it in what is together regarded as a desirable direction. Accomplishing this twin goal requires the active collaboration of researcher and client, and thus it stresses the importance of co-learning as a primary aspect of the research process."

What separates this type of research from general professional practices, consulting, or daily problem-solving is the emphasis on scientific study, which is to say the researcher studies the problem systematically and ensures the intervention is informed by theoretical considerations. Much of the researcher's time is spent on refining the methodological tools to suit the exigencies of the situation, and on collecting, analysing, and presenting data on an ongoing, cyclical basis.

Several attributes separate action research from other types of research. Primary is its focus on turning the people involved into researchers, too—people learn best, and more willingly apply what they have learned, when they do it themselves. It also has a social dimension—the research takes place in real-world situations, and aims to solve real problems. Finally, the initiating researcher, unlike in other disciplines, makes no attempt to remain objective, but openly acknowledges their bias to the other participants.

ACTION RESEARCH PROCESS

Stephen Kemmis has developed a simple model of the cyclical nature of the typical action research process. Each cycle has four steps: plan, act, observe, reflect.

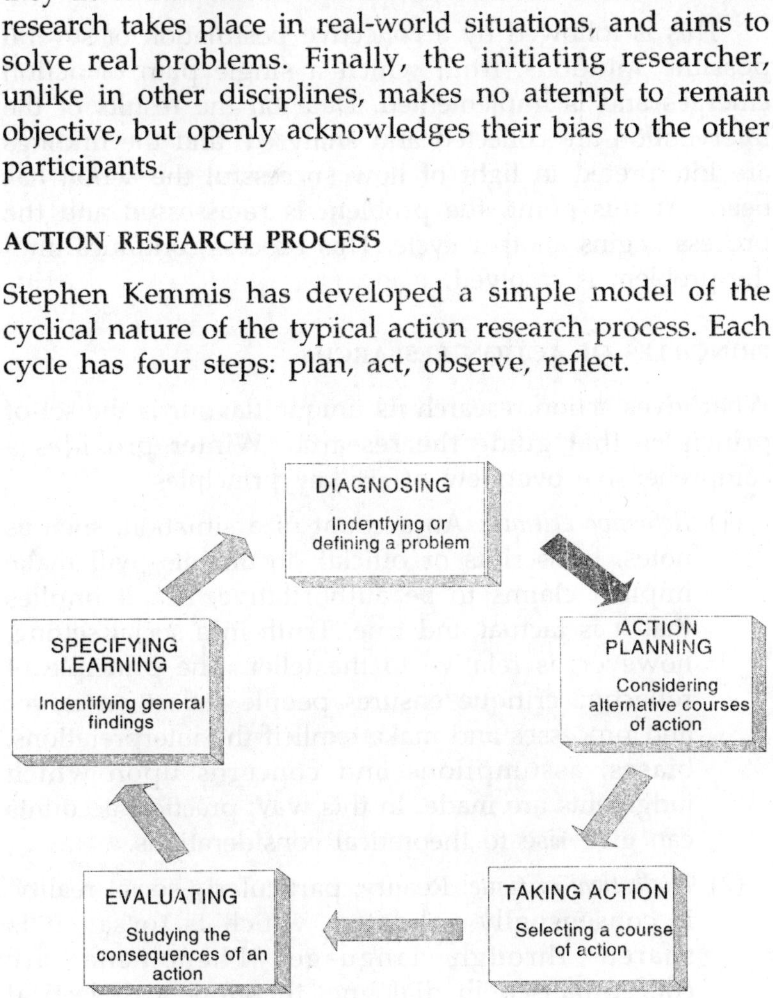

Figure 10.1. Action Research Model

Gerald Susman gives a somewhat more elaborate listing. He distinguishes five phases to be conducted within each research cycle (Figure 10.1). Initially, a problem is identified and data is collected for a more detailed diagnosis.

This is followed by a collective postulation of several possible solutions, from which a single plan of action emerges and is implemented. Data on the results of the intervention are collected and analysed, and the findings are interpreted in light of how successful the action has been. At this point, the problem is re-assessed and the process begins another cycle. This process continues until the problem is resolved.

PRINCIPLES OF ACTION RESEARCH

What gives action research its unique flavour is the set of principles that guide the research. Winter provides a comprehensive overview of six key principles.

(1) *Reflexive critique*: An account of a situation, such as notes, transcripts or official documents, will make implicit claims to be authoritative, i.e., it implies that it is factual and true. Truth in a social setting, however, is relative to the teller. The principle of reflective critique ensures people reflect on issues and processes and make explicit the interpretations, biases, assumptions and concerns upon which judgments are made. In this way, practical accounts can give rise to theoretical considerations.

(2) *Dialectical critique*: Reality, particularly social reality, is consensually validated, which is to say it is shared through language. Phenomena are conceptualised in dialogue, therefore a dialectical critique is required to understand the set of relationships both between the phenomenon and its context, and between the elements constituting the

phenomenon. The key elements to focus attention on are those constituent elements that are unstable, or in opposition to one another. These are the ones that are most likely to create changes.

(3) *Collaborative Resource*: Participants in an action research project are co-researchers. The principle of collaborative resource presupposes that each person's ideas are equally significant as potential resources for creating interpretive categories of analysis, negotiated among the participants. It strives to avoid the skewing of credibility stemming from the prior status of an idea-holder. It especially makes possible the insights gleaned from noting the contradictions both between many viewpoints and within a single viewpoint

(4) *Risk*: The change process potentially threatens all previously established ways of doing things, thus creating psychic fears among the practitioners. One of the more prominent fears comes from the risk to ego stemming from open discussion of one's interpretations, ideas, and judgments. Initiators of action research will use this principle to allay others' fears and invite participation by pointing out that they, too, will be subject to the same process, and that whatever the outcome, learning will take place.

(5) *Plural Structure*: The nature of the research embodies a multiplicity of views, commentaries and critiques, leading to multiple possible actions and interpretations. This plural structure of inquiry requires a plural text for reporting. This means that there will be many accounts made explicit, with commentaries on their contradictions, and a range of options for action presented. A report, therefore, acts as a support for ongoing discussion among collaborators, rather than a final conclusion of fact.

(6) *Theory, Practice, Transformation*: For action researchers, theory informs practice, practice refines theory, in a continuous transformation. In any setting, people's actions are based on implicitly held assumptions, theories and hypotheses, and with every observed result, theoretical knowledge is enhanced. The two are intertwined aspects of a single change process. It is up to the researchers to make explicit the theoretical justifications for the actions, and to question the bases of those justifications. The ensuing practical applications that follow are subjected to further analysis, in a transformative cycle that continuously alternates emphasis between theory and practice.

USES OF ACTION RESEARCH

Action research is used in real situations, rather than in contrived, experimental studies, since its primary focus is on solving real problems. It can, however, be used by social scientists for preliminary or pilot research, especially when the situation is too ambiguous to frame a precise research question. Mostly, though, in accordance with its principles, it is chosen when circumstances require flexibility, the involvement of the people in the research, or change must take place quickly or holistically.

It is often the case that those who apply this approach are practitioners who wish to improve understanding of their practice, social change activists trying to mount an action campaign, or, more likely, academics who have been invited into an organisation by decision-makers aware of a problem requiring action research, but lacking the requisite methodological knowledge to deal with it.

ACTION RESEARCH AND RESEARCH PARADIGM

Positivist Paradigm

The main research paradigm for the past several centuries has been that of Logical Positivism. This paradigm is based on a number of principles, including: a belief in an objective reality, knowledge of which is only gained from sense data that can be directly experienced and verified between independent observers.

Phenomena are subject to natural laws that humans discover in a logical manner through empirical testing, using inductive and deductive hypotheses derived from a body of scientific theory. Its methods rely heavily on quantitative measures, with relationships among variables commonly shown by mathematical means. Positivism, used in scientific and applied research, has been considered by many to be the antithesis of the principles of action research.

Interpretive Paradigm

Over the last half century, a new research paradigm has emerged in the social sciences to break out of the constraints imposed by positivism. With its emphasis on the relationship between socially-engendered concept formation and language, it can be referred to as the Interpretive paradigm.

Containing such qualitative methodological approaches as phenomenology, ethnography, and hermeneutics, it is characterised by a belief in a socially constructed, subjectively-based reality, one that is influenced by culture and history. Nonetheless it still retains the ideals of researcher objectivity, and researcher as passive collector and expert interpreter of data.

Paradigm of Praxis

Though sharing a number of perspectives with the interpretive paradigm, and making considerable use of its related qualitative methodologies, there are some researchers who feel that neither it nor the positivist paradigms are sufficient epistemological structures under which to place action research. Rather, a paradigm of Praxis is seen as where the main affinities lie. Praxis, a term used by Aristotle, is the art of acting upon the conditions one faces in order to change them. It deals with the disciplines and activities predominant in the ethical and political lives of people.

Aristotle contrasted this with Theoria—those sciences and activities that are concerned with knowing for its own sake. Both are equally needed he thought. That knowledge is derived from practice, and practice informed by knowledge, in an ongoing process, is a cornerstone of action research. Action researchers also reject the notion of researcher neutrality, understanding that the most active researcher is often one who has most at stake in resolving a problematic situation.

EVOLUTION OF ACTION RESEARCH

Kurt Lewin is generally considered the 'father' of action research. A German social and experimental psychologist, and one of the founders of the Gestalt school, he was concerned with social problems, and focused on participative group processes for addressing conflict, crises, and change, generally within organisations. Initially, he was associated with the Center for Group Dynamics at MIT in Boston, but soon went on to establish his own National Training Laboratories.

Lewin first coined the term 'action research' in his 1946 paper "Action Research and Minority Problems", characterising Action Research as "a comparative research on the conditions and effects of various forms of social action and research leading to social action", using a process of "a spiral of steps, each of which is composed of a circle of planning, action, and fact-finding about the result of the action". Eric Trist, another major contributor to the field from that immediate post-war era, was a social psychiatrist whose group at the Tavistock Institute of Human Relations in London engaged in applied social research, initially for the civil repatriation of German prisoners of war. He and his colleagues tended to focus more on large-scale, multi-organisational problems.

Both Lewin and Trist applied their research to systemic change in and between organisations. They emphasised direct professional—client collaboration and affirmed the role of group relations as basis for problem-solving. Both were avid proponents of the principle that decisions are best implemented by those who help make them.

TYPES OF ACTION RESEARCH

By the mid-1970s, the field had evolved, revealing 4 main 'streams' that had emerged: traditional, contextural (action learning), radical, and educational action research.

Traditional Action Research

Traditional Action Research stemmed from Lewin's work within organisations and encompasses the concepts and practices of Field Theory, Group Dynamics, T-Groups, and the Clinical Model. The growing importance of labour-management relations led to the application of action research in the areas of Organisation Development, Quality of Working Life (QWL), Socio-technical systems, and Organisational Democracy. This traditional approach tends toward the conservative, generally maintaining the status quo with regards to organisational power structures.

Contextural Action Research

Contextural Action Research, also sometimes referred to as Action Learning, is an approach derived from Trist's work on relations between organisations. It is contextural, insofar as it entails reconstituting the structural relations among actors in a social environment; domain-based, in that it tries to involve all affected parties and stakeholders; holographic, as each participant understands the working of the whole; and it stresses that participants act as project designers and co-researchers. The concept of organisational ecology, and the use of search conferences come out of contextural action research, which is more of a liberal philosophy, with social transformation occurring by consensus and normative incrementalism.

Radical Action Research

The Radical stream, which has its roots in Marxian 'dialectical materialism' and the praxis orientations of Antonio Gramsci, has a strong focus on emancipation and the overcoming of power imbalances. Participatory Action Research, often found in liberationist movements and international development circles, and Feminist Action Research both strive for social transformation via an advocacy process to strengthen peripheral groups in society.

Educational Action Research

A fourth stream, that of Educational Action Research, has its foundations in the writings of John Dewey, the great American educational philosopher of the 1920s and 30s, who believed that professional educators should become involved in community problem-solving. Its practitioners, not surprisingly, operate mainly out of educational institutions, and focus on development of curriculum, professional development, and applying learning in a social context. It is often the case that university-based action researchers work with primary and secondary school teachers and students on community projects.

Participatory Action Research

Participatory action research has emerged in recent years as a significant methodology for intervention, development and change within communities and groups. It is now promoted and implemented by many international development agencies and university programmes CCAR, as well as countless local community organisations around the world.

Participatory action research is a recognised form of experimental research that focuses on the effects of the researcher's direct actions of practice within a participatory community with the goal of improving the performance quality of the community or an area of concern. Action research involves utilising a systematic cyclical method of planning, taking action, observing, evaluating (including self-evaluation) and critical reflecting prior to planning the next cycle.

The actions have a set goal of addressing an identified problem in the workplace, for example, reducing the illiteracy of students through use of new strategies. It is a collaborative method to test new ideas and implement action for change. It involves direct participation in a dynamic research process, while monitoring and evaluating the effects of the researcher's actions with the aim of improving practice. At its core, action research is a way to increase understanding of how change in one's actions or practices can mutually benefit a community of practitioners. Understanding action research.

"Essentially Participatory Action Research (PAR) is research which involves all relevant parties in actively examining together current action (which they experience as problematic) in order to change and improve it. They do this by critically reflecting on the historical, political, cultural, economic, geographic and other contexts which make sense of it. ... Participatory action research is not just research which is hoped will be followed by action. It is action which is researched, changed and re-researched, within the research process by participants. Nor is it simply an exotic variant of consultation.

Instead, it aims to be active co-research, by and for those to be helped. Nor can it be used by one group of people to get another group of people to do what is thought best for them—whether that is to implement a central policy or an organisational or service change. Instead it tries to be a genuinely democratic or non-coercive process whereby those to be helped, determine the purposes and outcomes of their own inquiry."—Wadsworth, Y. What is Participatory Action Research?

The "research" aspects of PAR attempt to avoid the traditional "extractive" research carried out by universities and governments where "experts" go to a community, study their subjects, and take away their data to write their papers, reports and theses. Research in PAR is ideally BY the local people and FOR the local people. Research is designed to address specific issues identified by local people, and the results are directly applied to the problems at hand. PAR proceeds through repeated cycles, in which researchers and the community start with the identification of major issues, concerns and problems, initiate research, originate action, learn about this action and proceed to a new research and action cycle. This process is a continuous one.

Participants in Action Research projects continuously reflect on their learning from the actions and proceed to initiate new actions on the spot. Outcomes are very difficult to predict from the outset, challenges are sizeable and achievements depend to a very large extent on researcher's commitment, creativity and imagination. Examples of action research projects dissertations and masters thesis can be easily found by searching the internet. Some universities host sites where the best example of this form of research in corporate and university organisations, and school communities.

PAR should not be confused with PRA—Participatory rural appraisal. PRA is an assessment technique that could form part of a PAR process, but does not encompass the full action-reflection cycle. PAR has many of its roots in social psychology. It builds on the Action research and Group Dynamics models developed by psychologist Kurt Lewin in the early-to-mid 1900s, as well as on the study of oral culture by such scholars as Milman Parry and Walter J. Ong. At its core, PAR revolves around three sets of relationships: relations between individuals within communities and groups, relations between those groups and communities, and relations between people and their physical environment.

Management of group dynamics in its many aspects thus plays a central role in PAR processes, and PAR practitioners/facilitators must have a strong foundation in this field. PAR builds on the critical pedagogy put forward by Paulo Freire as a response to the traditional formal models of education where the "teacher" stands at the front and "imparts" information to the "students" that are passive recipients. This was further developed in "adult education" models throughout Latin America. Friere wrote,

> "The silenced are not just incidental to the curiosity of the researcher but are the masters of inquiry into the

> underlying causes of the events in their world. In this context research becomes a means of moving them beyond silence into a quest to proclaim the world."

Based on the work of Freire, it was Colombian sociologist Orlando Fals-Borda who gave PAR its worldwide recognition by organising the first PAR conferences in Cartagena, Colombia. Based on his research with peasant groups in rural Boyaca and with other underserved groups, Fals-Borda was able to effectively incorporate the "Community Action" component into the research plans of many traditionally trained researchers. It was not until then that communities started to fully appreciate the benefits of this approach which had initially seemed too abstract for many.

Antonio Gramsci is less known for, yet very important in contrtibuting to PAR. Gramsci, writing in early 20th century Italy, argued that all people are intellectuals and philosophers. "Organic intellectuals" is how he terms people who take their local knowledge from life experiences, and use that knowledge to address changes and problems in society. The idea that PAR researchers are really co-learners and researchers with the people they meet in the research process promotes the validity that all people are intellectuals who develop intricate philosophies through lived experience.

PAR also has its roots in phenomenology and postmodernism. These movements validated experience as a valid way of knowing, very much the foundation of the "action-reflection" model of Experiential learning and the PAR process. PAR is part of an important shift in paradigm from the traditional, positivist, science paradigm which arose to bring certainty and verifiability to research questions, to postpositivism which recognises and tries to address complex human and social problems.

Finally, PAR has origins within the development discourse.

PAR has evolved through the 1990s and into the 21st century as it has been applied to various fields within international development. For example, participatory plant breeding (PPB) and participatory technology development (PTD) are two techniques that utilise PAR approaches. More methods have been developed to add nuance and solidify key processes of "how" to do PAR, such as participatory development communication (PDC) and participatory video (PV).

Practitioners have also recently tried to move away from the word "research" because of its extractive connotations and abstract meaning to many community and group members. Thus new names are being used, such as "participatory action learning", "participatory learning-action", and "participatory action development". PAR is a popular method used in teaching adult learners in low-income communities, and others how to explore, challenge, and react to their own needs.

It is gaining popularity among community youth workers, as well as middle and senior high school teachers as a successful methodology for engaging youth voice in the classroom. According to Torre & Fine, "Youth PAR projects are typically centred on issues of intimate, structural violence: educational justice, access to quality healthcare, the criminalisation of youth, gang violence, police brutality, race/gender/sexuality oppression, gentrification and environmental issues." PAR is also increasingly used in service learning projects.

ACTION RESEARCH TOOLS

Action Research is more of a holistic approach to problem-solving, rather than a single method for collecting and analysing data. Thus, it allows for several different research tools to be used as the project is conducted. These various methods, which are generally common to the qualitative research paradigm, include: keeping a research journal, document collection and analysis, participant observation recordings, questionnaire surveys, structured and unstructured interviews, and case studies.

Search Conference

Of all of the tools utilised by action researchers, the one that has been developed exclusively to suit the needs of the action research approach is that of the search conference, initially developed by Eric Trist and Fred Emery at the Tavistock Institute in 1959, and first implemented for the merger of Bristol-Siddley Aircraft Engines in 1960.

The search conference format has seen widespread development since that time, with variations on Trist and Emery's theme becoming known under other names due to their promotion by individual academics and consultants. These include Dannemiller-Tyson's Interactive Strategic Planning, Marvin Weisbord's Future Search Conference, Dick Axelrod's Conference Model Redesign, Harrison Owen's Open Space, and ICA's Strategic Planning.

Search conferences also have been conducted for many different circumstances and participants, including: decision-makers from several countries visioning the "Future of Participative Democracy in the Americas"; practitioners and policymakers in the field of health promotion in Ontario taking charge in an era of cutbacks; and Xerox employees sorting out enterprise re-organisation.

Eric Trist sums up the process quite nicely—

> "Searching... is carried out in groups which are composed of the relevant stakeholders. The group meets under social island conditions for 2-3 days,

> sometimes as long as five. The opening sessions are concerned with elucidating the factors operating in the wider contextual environment—those producing the meta-problems and likely to affect the future. The content is contributed entirely by the members. The staff are facilitators only. Items are listed in the first instance without criticism in the plenary session and displayed on flip charts which surround the room. The material is discussed in greater depth in small groups and the composite picture checked out in plenary. The group next examines its own organisational setting or settings against this wider background and then proceeds to construct a picture of a desirable future. It is surprising how much agreement there often is. Only when all this has been done is consideration given to action steps..."

ACTION RESEARCHERS

Upon invitation into a domain, the outside researcher's role is to implement the Action Research method in such a manner as to produce a mutually agreeable outcome for all participants, with the process being maintained by them afterwards. To accomplish this, it may necessitate the adoption of many different roles at various stages of the process, including those of:

— Planner leader.

— Catalyser facilitator.

— Teacher designer.

— Listener observer.

— Synthesiser reporter.

The main role, however, is to nurture local leaders to the point where they can take responsibility for the process. This point is reached they understand the methods and are able to carry on when the initiating researcher leaves. In many Action Research situations, the hired researcher's role is primarily to take the time to facilitate dialogue and foster reflective analysis among the participants, provide them with periodic reports, and write a final report when the researcher's involvement has ended.

ETHICAL CONSIDERATIONS

Because action research is carried out in real-world circumstances, and involves close and open communication among the people involved, the researchers must pay close attention to ethical considerations in the conduct of their work. Richard Winter lists a number of principles:

- "Make sure that the relevant persons, committees and authorities have been consulted, and that the principles guiding the work are accepted in advance by all.
- All participants must be allowed to influence the work, and the wishes of those who do not wish to participate must be respected.
- The development of the work must remain visible and open to suggestions from others.
- Permission must be obtained before making observations or examining documents produced for other purposes.
- Descriptions of others' work and points of view must be negotiated with those concerned before being published.
- The researcher must accept responsibility for maintaining confidentiality."

To this might be added several more points:

- Decisions made about the direction of the research and the probable outcomes are collective.
- Researchers are explicit about the nature of the research process from the beginning, including all personal biases and interests.

— There is equal access to information generated by the process for all participants.

— The outside researcher and the initial design team must create a process that maximises the opportunities for involvement of all participants.

ACTION RESEARCH AND INFORMATION SYSTEMS

In the past ten years or so, there has been a marked increase in the number of organisations that are making use of information technology and computer mediated communications. This has led to a number of convergences between information systems and action research. In some cases, it has been a matter of managers of corporate networks employing action research techniques to facilitate large-scale changes to their information systems.

In others, it has been a question of community-based action research projects making use of computer communications to broaden participation. Much of the action research carried out over the past 40 years has been conducted in local settings with the participants meeting face-to-face with "real-time" dialogue. The emergence of the Internet has led to an explosion of asynchronous and aspatial group communication in the form of e-mail and computer conferences, and recently, v-mail and video conferencing.

While there have been numerous attempts to use this new technology in assisting group learning, both within organisations and among groups in the community, there is a dearth of published studies on the use of action research methods in such projects Lau and Hayward, in a recent review of the literature, found that most research on group support systems to date has been in short-term, experimental situations using quantitative methods. There are a few examples, though, of longitudinal studies in naturalistic settings using qualitative methods; of those that did use action research, none studied the use and effects of communication systems in groups and organisations.

We can now to turn to the case studies, both of which are situated in an area in need of more research—that of the use of information technology as a potentially powerful adjunct to action research processes. Lau and Hayward used an action research approach in a study of their own to explore the structuration of Internet-based collaborative work groups. Over a two-year period, the researchers participated as facilitators in three action research cycles of problem-solving among approximately 15 instructors and project staff, and 25 health professionals from various regions striving to make a transition to a more community-based health programme.

The aim was to explore how Internet-based communications would influence their evolution into a virtual collaborative workgroup. The first phase was taken up with defining expectations, providing the technology and developing the customised workgroup system. Feedback from participants noted that shorter and more spaced training sessions, with instructions more focused on specific projects would have been more helpful. The next phase saw the full deployment of the system, and the main lesson learned was that the steepness of the learning curve was severely underestimated, with frustrations only minimally satisfied by a great deal of technical support provided by telephone.

The final cycle saw the stabilisation of the system and the emergence of the virtual groups. The researchers found that those who used the system interactively were more likely to establish projects that were collaborative in nature, and that the lack of high quality information on community healthcare online was a drawback. The participants reported learning a great deal from the initiative. The interpretations of the study suggest that role clarity, relationship building, information sharing, resource support, and experiential learning are important aspects in virtual group development. There was also a sense that more research was needed on how group support systems can help groups interact with their external environment, as well as on how to enhance the process of learning by group members.

Comstock and Fox have written about their experiences in integrating computer conferencing into a learning community for mid-career working adults attending a Graduate Management Programme at Antioch University in Seattle. From 1992 to 1995, the researchers and their students made use of a dial-up computer conferencing system called Caucus to augment learning outside of monthly classroom weekends. Their findings relate to establishing boundaries to interaction, creating a caring community, and building collaborative learning. Boundary setting was a matter of both defined membership, i.e., access to particular conferences, and actual participation.

The architecture of the online environment was equated to that of a house, in which locked rooms allowed for privacy, but hampered interaction. They suggest some software design changes that would provide more cues and flexibility to improve access and usage. Relationships in a caring community were fostered by caring talk, personal conversations and story telling. Over time, expressions of personal concern for other participants increased, exemplifying a more tightly-knit group.

Playful conversations of a personal nature also improved group relations, as did stories of events in individuals' lives. These processes provided the support and induced the trust needed to sustain the more in-depth collaborative learning taking place. Students were expected to use the system for collaborative learning using three forms of conversation—dialogue, discussion and critical reflection.

Dialogues were enjoined as a result of attempts to relate classroom lessons to personal situations at work, with a better understanding provided by multiple opinions. Discussions, distinguished by the goal of making a group decision or taking an action, required a fair degree of moderation, insofar as participants found it difficult to reach closure. The process of reflecting critically on ideas was also difficult—participants rarely took the time to analyse postings, preferring a more immediate, and more superficial, conversational style.

The authors conclude with four recommendations:

(1) Be clear about the purpose of the computer conference and expectations for use.
(2) Develop incentives for widespread and continuous participation.
(3) Pay attention to affects of the software on the way the system is used for learning.
(4) Teach members of the community how to translate face-to-face collaborative processes to the on-line environment.

11

Quantitative and Qualitative Research Methods

The design of any study begins with the selection of a topic and a research methodology. These initial decisions reflect assumptions about the social world, how science should be conducted, and what constitutes legitimate problems, solutions, and criteria of "proof." Different approaches to research encompass both theory and method. Two general approaches are widely recognised: quantitative research and qualitative research. Quantitative research is an inquiry into an identified problem, based on testing a theory, measured with numbers, and analysed using statistical techniques.

The goal of quantitative methods is to determine whether the predictive generalisations of a theory hold true. It is important to be able to identify and understand the research approach underlying any given study because the selection of a research approach influences the questions asked, the methods chosen, the statistical analyses used, the inferences made, and the ultimate goal of the research. When critically reviewing scientific research, the questions asked, and the answers given, will differ depending upon whether the research is quantitative or qualitative.

QUANTITATIVE RESEARCH

Quantitative research is the systematic scientific investigation of quantitative properties and phenomena and their relationships. The objective of quantitative research is to develop and employ mathematical models, theories and/or hypotheses pertaining to natural phenomena. The process of measurement is central to quantitative research because it provides the fundamental connection between empirical observation and mathematical expression of quantitative relationships.

Quantitative research is widely used in both the natural sciences and social sciences, from physics and biology to sociology and journalism. It is also used as a way to research different aspects of education. The term quantitative research is most often used in the social sciences in contrast to qualitative research.

Quantitative research is often an iterative process whereby evidence is evaluated, theories and hypotheses are refined, technical advances are made, and so on. Virtually all research in physics is quantitative whereas research in other scientific disciplines, such as taxonomy and anatomy, may involve a combination of quantitative and other analytic approaches and methods.

In the social sciences particularly, quantitative research is often contrasted with qualitative research which is the examination, analysis and interpretation of observations for the purpose of discovering underlying meanings and patterns of relationships, including classifications of types of phenomena and entities, in a manner that does not involve mathematical models.

Approaches to quantitative psychology were first modelled on quantitative approaches in the physical sciences by Gustav Fechner in his work on psychophysics, which built on the work of Ernst Heinrich Weber. Although a distinction is commonly drawn between qualitative and quantitative aspects of scientific investigation, it has been argued that the two go hand in hand.

For example, based on analysis of the history of science, Kuhn concludes that "large amounts of qualitative work have usually been prerequisite to fruitful quantification in the physical sciences". Qualitative research is often used to gain a general sense of phenomena and to form theories that can be tested using further quantitative research. For instance, in the social sciences qualitative research methods are often used to gain better understanding of such things as intentionality and meaning.

Statistics in Quantitative Research

Statistics is the most widely used branch of mathematics in quantitative research outside of the physical sciences, and also finds applications within the physical sciences, such as in statistical mechanics. Statistical methods are used extensively within fields such as economics, social sciences and biology. Quantitative research using statistical methods typically begins with the collection of data based on a theory or hypothesis, followed by the application of descriptive or inferential statistical methods.

Causal relationships are studied by manipulating factors thought to influence the phenomena of interest while controlling other variables relevant to the experimental outcomes. In the field of health, for example, researchers might measure and study the relationship between dietary intake and measurable physiological effects such as weight loss, controlling for other key variables such as exercise. Quantitatively based opinion surveys are widely used in the media, with statistics such as the proportion of respondents in favour of a position commonly reported.

In opinion surveys, respondents are asked a set of structured questions and their responses are tabulated. In the field of climate science, researchers compile and compare statistics such as temperature or atmospheric concentrations of carbon dioxide. Empirical relationships and associations are also frequently studied by using some form of General linear model, non-linear model, or by using factor analysis.

A fundamental principle in quantitative research is that correlation does not imply causation. This principle follows from the fact that it is always possible a spurious relationship exists for variables between which covariance is found in some degree. Associations may be examined between any combination of continuous and categorical variables using methods of statistics.

Measurement in Quantitative Research

Views regarding the role of measurement in quantitative research are somewhat divergent. Measurement is often regarded as being only a means by which observations are expressed numerically in order to investigate causal relations or associations. However, it has been argued that measurement often plays a more important role in quantitative research. For example, Thomas Kuhn argued that results which appear anomalous in the context of accepted theory potentially lead to the genesis of a search for a new, natural phenomenon. He believed that such anomalies are most striking when encountered during the process of obtaining measurements, as reflected in the following observations regarding the function of measurement in science:

When measurement departs from theory, it is likely to yield mere numbers, and their very neutrality makes them particularly sterile as a source of remedial suggestions. But numbers register the departure from theory with an authority and finesse that no qualitative technique can duplicate, and that departure is often enough to start a search. In classical physics, the theory and definitions which underpin measurement are generally deterministic in nature. In contrast, probabilistic measurement models known as the Rasch model and Item response theory models are generally employed in the social sciences.

Psychometrics is the field of study concerned with the theory and technique for measuring social and psychological attributes and phenomena. This field is central to much quantitative research that is undertaken within the social sciences. Quantitative research may involve the use of proxies as stand-ins for other quantities that cannot be directly measured. Tree-ring width, for example, is considered a reliable proxy of ambient environmental conditions such as the warmth of growing seasons or amount of rainfall.

Although scientists cannot directly measure the temperature of past years, tree-ring width and other climate proxies have been used to provide a semi-quantitative record of average temperature in the Northern Hemisphere back to 1000 A.D. When used in this way, the proxy record (tree ring width, say) only reconstructs a certain amount of the variance of the original record.

The proxy may be calibrated to determine how much variation is captured, including whether both short and long term variation is revealed. In the case of tree-ring width, different species in different places may show more or less sensitivity to, say, rainfall or temperature: when reconstructing a temperature record there is considerable skill in selecting proxies that are well correlated with the desired variable.

Quantitative Methods

Quantitative methods are research techniques that are used to gather quantitative data—information dealing with numbers and anything that is measurable. Statistics, tables and graphs, are often used to present the results of these methods. They are therefore to be distinguished from qualitative methods. In most physical and biological sciences, the use of either quantitative or qualitative methods is uncontroversial, and each is used when appropriate.

In the social sciences, particularly in sociology, social anthropology and psychology, the use of one or other type of method has become a matter of controversy and even ideology, with particular schools of thought within each discipline favouring one type of method and pouring scorn on to the other. Advocates of quantitative methods argue that only by using such methods can the social sciences become truly scientific; advocates of qualitative methods argue that quantitative methods tend to obscure the reality of the social phenomena under study because they underestimate or neglect the non-measurable factors, which may be the most important.

The modern tendency is to use eclectic approaches. Quantitative methods might be used with a global qualitative frame. Qualitative methods might be used to understand the meaning of the numbers produced by quantitative methods. Using quantitative methods, it is possible to give precise and testable expression to qualitative ideas. This combination of quantitative and qualitative data gathering is often referred to as mixed-methods research.

QUALITATIVE RESEARCH

Qualitative research is a field of inquiry that crosscuts disciplines and subject matters. Qualitative researchers aim to acquire an in-depth understanding of human behaviour and the reasons that govern human behaviour. Qualitative research relies on reasons behind various aspects of behaviour. Simply put, it investigates the why and how of decision-making, not just what, where, and when. Hence, the need is for smaller but focused samples rather than large random samples, which qualitative research categorises data into patterns as the primary basis for organising and reporting results. Qualitative researchers typically rely on four methods for gathering information:

(1) Participation in the setting.

(2) Direct observation.

(3) In depth interviews.

(4) Analysis of documents and materials.

The term qualitative research is most often used in the social sciences in contrast to quantitative research. Qualitative research was one of the first forms of social studies, but in the 1950s and 1960s when quantitative science reached its peak of popularity, it was diminished in importance and began to regain recognition as late as in the 1970s. The phrase 'qualitative research' was until then restricted as a discipline of anthropology or sociology, and terms like ethnography, fieldwork, participant observation and Chicago school were used instead.

During the 1970s and 1980s qualitative research began to be used in other disciplines, and became a significant type of research in the fields of education studies, social work studies, women's studies, disability studies, information studies, management studies, nursing service studies, human service studies, psychology, communication studies, and other. Some qualitative research occurred in the consumer products industry during this period: researchers most interested in investigating consumer new product and product positioning opportunities worked with a handful of the earliest consumer research pioneers including Gene Reilly of The Gene Reilly Group in Darien, CT, Jerry Schoenfeld of Gerald Schoenfeld & Partners in Tarrytown, NY and Martin Calle of Calle & Company, Greenwich, CT.

In the late 1980s and 1990s after a spate of criticisms from the quantitative side, paralleling a slowdown in traditional media spending for the decade, new methods of qualitative research evolved, to address the perceived problems with reliability and imprecise modes of data analysis. One way of differentiating Qualitative research from Quantitative research is that largely Qualitative research is exploratory, while Quantitative research hopes to be conclusive. However it may be argued that each reflects a particular discourse; neither being definitively more conclusive or 'true' than the other.

Quantitative data are of the kind that may lead to measurement or other kinds of analysis involving applied mathematics, while Qualitative data cannot necessarily be put into a context that can be graphed or displayed as a mathematical term. Qualitative researchers may use different approaches, such as the grounded theory practice, narratology, storytelling, classical ethnography, or shadowing. Qualitative methods are also loosely present in other methodological approaches, such as action research or actor-network theory.

Contemporary qualitative studies are sometimes supported by computer programmes, such as MAXQDA and NVivo, although the benefits of software use are mainly in storing and segregating data, rather than in processing or analysing them. Although it is common in the social sciences to draw a distinction between qualitative and quantitative aspects of scientific investigation, it has been argued that the two may go hand in hand. For example, based on analysis of the history of science, Kuhn concluded "large amounts of qualitative work have usually been prerequisite to fruitful quantification in the physical sciences". Qualitative research is, in some cases, instrumental to developing an understanding of phenomena as a basis for quantitative research. Similarly, quantitative research may inform, or be drawn upon in the process of qualitative research.

Research Paradigms

There are three basic research paradigms — positivism (quantitative, scientific approach), interpretivism, and critical science. Positivism, or the scientific approach, we have explored in the early parts of this course. Critical science, or the critical approach, explores the social world, critiques it, and seeks to empower the individual to overcome problems in the social world. Critical science enables people to understand how society functions and methods by which unsatisfactory aspects can be changed. We do not cover critical science in this course.

Interpretivism, or the qualitative approach, is a way to gain insights through discovering meanings by improving our comprehension of the whole. Qualitative research explores the richness, depth, and complexity of phenomena. Qualitative research, broadly defined, means "any kind of research that produces findings not arrived at by means of statistical procedures or other means of quantification". Although acceptance of interpretivism is increasing within human movement sciences, positivism remains the dominant paradigm, as it does in other social science fields.

Assumptions of Interpretivism

The underlying assumption of interpretivism is that the whole needs to be examined in order to understand a phenomena. Interpretivism is critical of the positivism because it seeks to collect and analyse data from parts of a phenomena and, in so doing, positivism can miss important aspects of a comprehensive understanding of the whole.

Interpretivism proposes that there are multiple realities, not single realities of phenomena, and that these realities can differ across time and place. Unlike quantitative research, there is no overarching framework for how qualitative research should be conducted; rather each type of qualitative research is guided by particular philosophical stances that are taken in relation by the research to each phenomenon.

Types of Qualitative Research

The main types of qualitative research are:

— *Case study*: Attempts to shed light on a phenomena by studying indepth a single case example of the phenomena. The case can be an individual person, an event, a group, or an institution.

— *Grounded theory*: Theory is developed inductively from a corpus of data acquired by a participant-observer.

— *Phenomenology*: Describes the structures of experience as they present themselves to consciousness, without recourse to theory, deduction, or assumptions from other disciplines

— *Ethnography*: Focuses on the sociology of meaning through close field observation of sociocultural phenomena. Typically, the ethnographer focuses on a community.

— *Historical*: Systematic collection and objective evaluation of data related to past occurrences in order to test hypotheses concerning causes, effects, or trends of these events that may help to explain present events and anticipate future events.

Those who are not familiar with qualitative methodology may be surprised by the sheer volume of data and the detailed level of analysis that results even when research is confined to a small number of subjects. There are three main methods of data collection:

— *Interactive interviewing*: People asked to verbally described their experiences of phenomenon.

— *Written descriptions by participants:* People asked to write descriptions of their experiences of phenomenon.

— *Observation*: Descriptive observations of verbal and non-verbal behaviour.

Analysis begins when the data is first collected and is used to guide decisions related to further data collection. Qualitative studies are tools used in understanding and describing the world of human experience. Since we maintain our humanity throughout the research process, it is largely impossible to escape the subjective experience, even for the most seasoned of researchers. As we proceed through the research process, our humanness informs us and often directs us through such subtleties as intuition or 'aha' moments.

Speaking about the world of human experience requires an extensive commitment in terms of time and dedication to process; however, this world is often dismissed as 'subjective' and regarded with suspicion. This chapter acknowledges that small qualitative studies are not generalisable in the traditional sense, yet have redeeming qualities that set them above that requirement.

A major strength of the qualitative approach is the depth to which explorations are conducted and descriptions are written, usually resulting in sufficient details for the reader to grasp the idiosyncracies of the situation. The ultimate aim of qualitative research is to offer a perspective of a situation and provide well-written research reports that reflect the researcher's ability to illustrate or describe the corresponding phenomenon. One of the greatest strengths of the qualitative approach is the richness and depth of explorations and descriptions.

12

Analysis

By the time you get to the analysis of your data, most of the really difficult work has been done. It's much more difficult to: define the research problem; develop and implement a sampling plan; conceptualise, operationalise and test your measures; and develop a design structure. If you have done this work well, the analysis of the data is usually a fairly straightforward affair.

In most social research the data analysis involves three major steps, done in roughly this order:

— Cleaning and organising the data for analysis (Data Preparation).

— Describing the data (Descriptive Statistics).

— Testing Hypotheses and Models (Inferential Statistics).

Data Preparation involves checking or logging the data in; checking the data for accuracy; entering the data into the computer; transforming the data; and developing and documenting a database structure that integrates the various measures. Descriptive Statistics are used to describe the basic features of the data in a study. They provide simple summaries about the sample and the measures. Together with simple graphics analysis, they form the basis of virtually every quantitative analysis of data. With descriptive statistics you are simply describing what is, what the data shows.

Inferential Statistics investigate questions, models and hypotheses. In many cases, the conclusions from inferential statistics extend beyond the immediate data alone. For instance, we use inferential statistics to try to infer from the sample data what the population thinks. Or, we use inferential statistics to make judgments of the probability that an observed difference between groups is a dependable one or one that might have happened by chance in this study. Thus, we use inferential statistics to make inferences from our data to more general conditions; we use descriptive statistics simply to describe what's going on in our data.

In most research studies, the analysis section follows these three phases of analysis. Descriptions of how the data were prepared tend to be brief and to focus on only the more unique aspects to your study, such as specific data transformations that are performed. The descriptive statistics that you actually look at can be voluminous.

Usually, the researcher links each of the inferential analyses to specific research questions or hypotheses that were raised in the introduction, or notes any models that were tested that emerged as part of the analysis. In most analysis write-ups it's especially critical to not "miss the forest for the trees." If you present too much detail, the reader may not be able to follow the central line of the results. Often extensive analysis details are appropriately relegated to appendices, reserving only the most critical analysis summaries for the body of the report itself.

CONCLUSION VALIDITY

Of the four types of validity (internal validity, construct validity and external validity) conclusion validity is undoubtedly the least considered and most misunderstood. That's probably due to the fact that it was originally labelled 'statistical' conclusion validity and you know how even the mere mention of the word statistics will scare off most of the human race! In many ways, conclusion validity is the most important of the four validity types because it is relevant whenever we are trying to decide if there is a relationship in our observations. Perhaps we should start with an attempt at a definition:

> Conclusion validity is the degree to which conclusions we reach about relationships in our data are reasonable.

For instance, if we're doing a study that looks at the relationship between socioeconomic status (SES) and attitudes about capital punishment, we eventually want to reach some conclusion. Based on our data, we may conclude that there is a positive relationship, that persons with higher SES tend to have a more positive view of capital punishment while those with lower SES tend to be more opposed. Conclusion validity is the degree to which the conclusion we reach is credible or believable.

Although conclusion validity was originally thought to be a statistical inference issue, it has become more apparent that it is also relevant in qualitative research. For example, in an observational field study of homeless adolescents the researcher might, on the basis of field notes, see a pattern that suggests that teenagers on the street who use drugs are more likely to be involved in more complex social networks and to interact with a more varied group of people.

Although this conclusion or inference may be based entirely on impressionistic data, we can ask whether it has conclusion validity, that is, whether it is a reasonable conclusion about a relationship in our observations.

Whenever you investigate a relationship, you essentially have two possible conclusions—either there is a relationship in your data or there isn't. In either case, however, you could be wrong in your conclusion.

You might conclude that there is a relationship when in fact there is not, or you might infer that there isn't a relationship when in fact there is. So, we have to consider all of these possibilities when we talk about conclusion validity. It's important to realise that conclusion validity is an issue whenever you conclude there is a relationship, even when the relationship is between some programme and some outcome. In other words, conclusion validity also pertains to causal relationships.

Conclusion validity is only concerned with whether there is a relationship. For instance, in a programme evaluation, we might conclude that there is a positive relationship between our educational programme and achievement test scores—students in the programme get higher scores and students not in the programme get lower ones. Conclusion validity is essentially whether that relationship is a reasonable one or not, given the data. But it is possible that we will conclude that, while there is a relationship between the programme and outcome, the programme didn't cause the outcome. Perhaps some other factor, and not our programme, was responsible for the outcome in this study.

For instance, the observed differences in the outcome could be due to the fact that the programme group was smarter than the comparison group to begin with. Our observed posttest differences between these groups could be due to this initial difference and not be the result of our programme. This issue—the possibility that some other factor than our programme caused the outcome—is what internal validity is all about. So, it is possible that in a study we can conclude that our programme and outcome are related and also conclude that the outcome was caused by some factor other than the programme.

Here are some general guidelines you can follow in designing your study that will help improve conclusion validity.

— *Good Statistical Power*: The rule of thumb in social research is that you want statistical power to be greater than 0.8 in value. That is, you want to have at least 80 chances out of 100 of finding a relationship when there is one. As pointed out in the discussion of statistical power, there are several factors that interact to affect power. One thing you can usually do is to collect more information—use a larger sample size. Of course, you have to weigh the gain in power against the time and expense of having more participants or gathering more data. The second thing you can do is to increase your risk of making a Type I error—increase the chance that you will find a relationship when it's not there. In practical terms you can do that statistically by raising the alpha level. For instance, instead of using a 0.05 significance level, you might use 0.10 as your cutoff point. Finally, you can increase the effect size. Since the effect size is a ratio of the signal of the relationship to the noise in the context, there are two broad strategies here. To up the signal, you can increase the salience of the relationship itself. This is especially true in experimental contexts where you are looking at the effects of a programme or treatment. If you increase the dosage of the programme, it will be easier to see the effect when the treatment is stronger. The other option is to decrease the noise.

— *Good Reliability*: Reliability is related to the idea of noise or "error" that obscures your ability to see a relationship. In general, you can improve reliability by doing a better job of constructing measurement instruments, by increasing the number of questions on an scale or by reducing situational distractions in the measurement context.

— *Good Implementation*: When you are studying the effects of interventions, treatments or programmes, you can improve conclusion validity by assuring good implementation. This can be accomplished by training programme operators and standardising the protocols for administering the programme.

IDEA OF STATISTICAL POWER

One of the most interesting introductions to the idea of statistical power is given in the 'OJ' Page which was created by Rob Becker to illustrate how the decision a jury has to reach is similar to the decision a researcher makes when assessing a relationship. The OJ Page uses the infamous OJ Simpson murder trial in USA, to introduce the idea of statistical power and illustrate how manipulating various factors affects the validity of the verdict.

There are four interrelated components that influence the conclusions you might reach from a statistical test in a research project. The logic of statistical inference with respect to these components is often difficult to understand and explain. This paper attempts to clarify the four components and describe their interrelationships.

The four components are:

— Sample size, or the number of units accessible to the study.

— Effect size, or the salience of the treatment relative to the noise in measurement.

— Alpha level, or the odds that the observed result is due to chance.

— Power, or the odds that you will observe a treatment effect when it occurs.

Given values for any three of these components, it is possible to compute the value of the fourth. For instance, you might want to determine what a reasonable sample size would be for a study. If you could make reasonable estimates of the effect size, alpha level and power, it would be simple to compute the sample size. Some of these components will be more manipulable than others depending on the circumstances of the project.

For example, if the project is an evaluation of an educational programme or counseling programme with a specific number of available consumers, the sample size is set or predetermined. Or, if the drug dosage in a programme has to be small due to its potential negative side effects, the effect size may consequently be small. The goal is to achieve a balance of the four components that allows the maximum level of power to detect an effect if one exists, given programmematic, logistical or financial constraints on the other components.

DATA PREPARATION

Data Preparation involves checking or logging the data in; checking the data for accuracy; entering the data into the computer; transforming the data; and developing and documenting a database structure that integrates the various measures.

Logging the Data

In any research project you may have data coming from a number of different sources at different times:

— Mail surveys returns.

— Coded interview data.

— Pretest or posttest data.

— Observational data.

In all but the simplest of studies, you need to set up a procedure for logging the information and keeping track of it until you are ready to do a comprehensive data analysis. Different researchers differ in how they prefer to keep track of incoming data. In most cases, you will want to set up a database that enables you to assess at any time what data is already in and what is still outstanding. You could do this with any standard computerised database programme, although this requires familiarity with such programmes. or, you can accomplish this using standard statistical programmes and running simple descriptive analyses to get reports on data status.

It is also critical that the data analyst retain the original data records for a reasonable period of time—returned surveys, field notes, test protocols, and so on. Most professional researchers will retain such records for at least 5-7 years. For important or expensive studies, the original data might be stored in a data archive. The data analyst should always be able to trace a result from a data analysis back to the original forms on which the data was collected. A database for logging incoming data is a critical component in good research record-keeping.

Checking the Data

As soon as data is received you should screen it for accuracy. In some circumstances doing this right away will allow you to go back to the sample to clarify any problems or errors. There are several questions you should ask as part of this initial data screening:

— Are the responses legible/readable?

— Are all important questions answered?

— Are the responses complete?

— Is all relevant contextual information included?

In most social research, quality of measurement is a major issue. Assuring that the data collection process does not contribute inaccuracies will help assure the overall quality of subsequent analyses.

Database Structure

The database structure is the manner in which you intend to store the data for the study so that it can be accessed in subsequent data analyses. You might use the same structure you used for logging in the data or, in large complex studies, you might have one structure for logging data and another for storing it. As mentioned above, there are generally two options for storing data on computer—database programmes and statistical programmes.

Usually database programmes are the more complex of the two to learn and operate, but they allow the analyst greater flexibility in manipulating the data. In every research project, you should generate a printed codebook that describes the data and indicates where and how it can be accessed. Minimally the codebook should include the following items for each variable:

— Variable name.
— Variable description.
— Variable format (number, data, text).
— Instrument/method of collection.
— Date collected.
— Respondent or group.
— Variable location (in database).
— Notes.

The codebook is an indispensable tool for the analysis team. Together with the database, it should provide comprehensive documentation that enables other researchers who might subsequently want to analyse the data to do so without any additional information.

Data Entering

There are a wide variety of ways to enter the data into the computer for analysis. Probably the easiest is to just type the data in directly. In order to assure a high level of data accuracy, the analyst should use a procedure called double entry. In this procedure you enter the data once. Then, you use a special programme that allows you to enter the data a second time and checks each second entry against the first. If there is a discrepancy, the programme notifies the user and allows the user to determine the correct entry. This double entry procedure significantly reduces entry errors.

However, these double entry programmes are not widely available and require some training. An alternative is to enter the data once and set up a procedure for checking the data for accuracy. For instance, you might spot check records on a random basis. Once the data have been entered, you will use various programmes to summarise the data that allow you to check that all the data are within acceptable limits and boundaries. For instance, such summaries will enable you to easily spot whether there are persons whose age is 601 or who have a 7 entered where you expect a 1-to-5 response.

Data Transformations

Once the data have been entered it is almost always necessary to transform the raw data into variables that are usable in the analyses. There are a wide variety of transformations that you might perform. Some of the more common are:

Missing Values

Many analysis programmes automatically treat blank values as missing. In others, you need to designate specific values to represent missing values. For instance, you might use a value of -99 to indicate that the item is missing. You need to check the specific programme you are using to determine how to handle missing values.

Item Reversals

On scales and surveys, we sometimes use reversal items to help reduce the possibility of a response set. When you analyse the data, you want all scores for scale items to be in the same direction where high scores mean the same thing and low scores mean the same thing. In these cases, you have to reverse the ratings for some of the scale items. For instance, let's say you had a five point response scale for a self esteem measure where 1 meant strongly disagree and 5 meant strongly agree. One item is "I generally feel good about myself." If the respondent strongly agrees with this item they will put a 5 and this value would be indicative of higher self esteem.

Alternatively, consider an item like "Sometimes I feel like I'm not worth much as a person." Here, if a respondent strongly agrees by rating this a 5 it would indicate low self-esteem. To compare these two items, we would reverse the scores of one of them. We want a transformation where if the original value was 1 it's changed to 5, 2 is changed to 4, 3 remains the same, 4 is changed to 2 and 5 is changed to 1. While you could programme these changes as separate statements in most programme, it's easier to do this with a simple formula like:

New Value = (High Value + 1)—Original Value

In our example, the High Value for the scale is 5, so to get the new (transformed) scale value, we simply subtract each Original Value from 6 (i.e., 5 + 1).

Scale Totals

Once you've transformed any individual scale items you will often want to add or average across individual items to get a total score for the scale.

Categories

For many variables you will want to collapse them into categories. For instance, you may want to collapse income estimates into income ranges.

Descriptive Statistics

Descriptive statistics are used to describe the basic features of the data in a study. They provide simple summaries about the sample and the measures. Together with simple graphics analysis, they form the basis of virtually every quantitative analysis of data. Descriptive statistics are typically distinguished from inferential statistics. With descriptive statistics you are simply describing what is or what the data shows. With inferential statistics, you are trying to reach conclusions that extend beyond the immediate data alone.

For instance, we use inferential statistics to try to infer from the sample data what the population might think. Or, we use inferential statistics to make judgements of the probability that an observed difference between groups is a dependable one or one that might have happened by chance in this study. Thus, we use inferential statistics to make inferences from our data to more general conditions; we use descriptive statistics simply to describe what's going on in our data.

Descriptive Statistics are used to present quantitative descriptions in a manageable form. In a research study we may have lots of measures. Or we may measure a large number of people on any measure. Descriptive statistics help us to simply large amounts of data in a sensible way. Each descriptive statistic reduces lots of data into a simpler summary. For instance, consider a simple number used to summarise how well a batter is performing in baseball, the batting average. This single number is simply the number of hits divided by the number of times at bat.

A batter who is hitting .333 is getting a hit one time in every three at bats. One batting .250 is hitting one time in four. The single number describes a large number of discrete events. Or, consider the scourge of many students, the Grade Point Average (GPA). This single number describes the general performance of a student across a potentially wide range of course experiences. Every time you try to describe a large set of observations with a single indicator you run the risk of distorting the original data or losing important detail.

The batting average doesn't tell you whether the batter is hitting home runs or singles. It doesn't tell whether she's been in a slump or on a streak. The GPA doesn't tell you whether the student was in difficult courses or easy ones, or whether they were courses in their major field or in other disciplines. Even given these limitations, descriptive statistics provide a powerful summary that may enable comparisons across people or other units.

Univariate Analysis

Univariate analysis involves the examination across cases of one variable at a time. There are three major characteristics of a single variable that we tend to look at:

— The distribution.

— The central tendency.

— The dispersion.

Distributions may also be displayed using percentages. For example, you could use percentages to describe the:

— Percentage of people in different income levels.

— Percentage of people in different age ranges.

— Percentage of people in different ranges of standardised test scores.

Central Tendency: The central tendency of a distribution is an estimate of the "centre" of a distribution of values. There are three major types of estimates of central tendency:

— Mean.

— Median.

— Mode.

The Mean or average is probably the most commonly used method of describing central tendency. To compute the mean all you do is add up all the values and divide by the number of values. For example, the mean or average quiz score is determined by summing all the scores and dividing by the number of students taking the exam. For example, consider the test score values:

15, 20, 21, 20, 36, 15, 25, 15.

The sum of these 8 values is 167, so the mean is 167/8 = 20.875. The Median is the score found at the exact middle of the set of values. One way to compute the median is to list all scores in numerical order, and then locate the score in the centre of the sample. For example, if there are 500 scores in the list, score #250 would be the median. If we order the 8 scores shown above, we would get:

15,15,15,20,20,21,25,36

There are 8 scores and score #4 and #5 represent the halfway point. Since both of these scores are 20, the median is 20. If the two middle scores had different values, you would have to interpolate to determine the median. The mode is the most frequently occurring value in the set of scores. To determine the mode, you might again order the scores as shown above, and then count each one. The most frequently occurring value is the mode. In our example, the value 15 occurs three times and is the model.

In some distributions there is more than one modal value. For instance, in a bimodal distribution there are two values that occur most frequently. Notice that for the same set of 8 scores we got three different values—20.875, 20, and 15—for the mean, median and mode respectively. If the distribution is truly normal, the mean, median and mode are all equal to each other.

Dispersion: Dispersion refers to the spread of the values around the central tendency. There are two common measures of dispersion, the range and the standard deviation. The range is simply the highest value minus the lowest value. In our example distribution, the high value is 36 and the low is 15, so the range is 36 - 15 = 21. The Standard Deviation is a more accurate and detailed estimate of dispersion because an outlier can greatly exaggerate the range. The Standard Deviation shows the relation that set of scores has to the mean of the sample.

Inferential Statistics

With inferential statistics, you are trying to reach conclusions that extend beyond the immediate data alone. For instance, we use inferential statistics to try to infer from the sample data what the population might think. Or, we use inferential statistics to make judgements of the probability that an observed difference between groups is a dependable one or one that might have happened by chance in this study. Thus, we use inferential statistics to make inferences from our data to more general conditions; we use descriptive statistics simply to describe what's going on in our data.

Perhaps one of the simplest inferential test is used when you want to compare the average performance of two groups on a single measure to see if there is a difference. You might want to know whether eighth-grade boys and girls differ in math test scores or whether a programme group differs on the outcome measure from a control group. Whenever you wish to compare the average performance between two groups you should consider the t-test for differences between groups.

Most of the major inferential statistics come from a general family of statistical models known as the General Linear Model. This includes the t-test, Analysis of Variance (ANOVA), Analysis of Covariance (ANCOVA), regression analysis, and many of the multivariate methods like factor analysis, multidimensional scaling, cluster analysis, discriminant function analysis, and so on. Given the importance of the General Linear Model, it's a good idea for any serious social researcher to become familiar with its workings. One of the keys to understanding how groups are compared is embodied in the notion of the "dummy" variable. The name doesn't suggest that we are using variables that aren't very smart or, even worse, that the analyst who uses them is a "dummy"! Perhaps these variables would be better described as "proxy" variables.

Essentially a dummy variable is one that uses discrete numbers, usually 0 and 1, to represent different groups in your study. Dummy variables are a simple idea that enable some pretty complicated things to happen. One of the most important analyses in programme outcome evaluations involves comparing the programme and non-programme group on the outcome variable or variables. How we do this depends on the research design we use, research designs are divided into two major types of designs: experimental and quasi-experimental. Because the analyses differ for each, they are presented separately.

Experimental Analysis: The simple two-group post-test-only randomised experiment is usually analysed with the simple t-test or one-way ANOVA. The factorial experimental designs are usually analysed with the Analysis of Variance (ANOVA) Model. Randomised Block Designs use a special form of ANOVA blocking model that uses dummy-coded variables to represent the blocks. The Analysis of Covariance Experimental Design uses, not surprisingly, the Analysis of Covariance statistical model.

Quasi-Experimental Analysis: The quasi-experimental designs differ from the experimental ones in that they don't use random assignment to assign units to programme groups. The lack of random assignment in these designs tends to complicate their analysis considerably. For example, to analyse the Nonequivalent Groups Design (NEGD) we have to adjust the pretest scores for measurement error in what is often called a Reliability-Corrected Analysis of Covariance model. In the Regression-Discontinuity Design, we need to be especially concerned about curvilinearity and model misspecification.

Consequently, we tend to use a conservative analysis approach that is based on polynomial regression that starts by overfitting the likely true function and then reducing the model based on the results. The Regression Point Displacement Design has only a single treated unit. Nevertheless, the analysis of the RPD design is based directly on the traditional ANCOVA model. When you've investigated these various analytic models, you'll see that they all come from the same family—the General Linear Model. An understanding of that model will go a long way to introducing you to the intricacies of data analysis in applied and social research contexts.

The T-Test

The t-test assesses whether the means of two groups are statistically different from each other. This analysis is appropriate whenever you want to compare the means of two groups, and especially appropriate as the analysis for the posttest-only two-group randomised experimental design.

Dummy Variables

A dummy variable is a numerical variable used in regression analysis to represent subgroups of the sample in your study. In research design, a dummy variable is often used to distinguish different treatment groups. In the simplest case, we would use a 0,1 dummy variable where a person is given a value of 0 if they are in the control group or a 1 if they are in the treated group. Dummy variables are useful because they enable us to use a single regression equation to represent multiple groups. This means that we don't need to write out separate equation models for each subgroup. The dummy variables act like 'switches' that turn various parameters on and off in an equation. Another advantage of a 0,1 dummy-coded variable is that even though it is a nominal-level variable you can treat it statistically like an interval-level variable.

13

Report Writing

Developing a good, effective and concise report is an art form in itself. And, in many research projects you will need to write multiple reports that present the results at different levels of detail for different audiences.

There are several general considerations to keep in mind when generating a report:

— *The Audience:* Who is going to read the report? Reports will differ considerably depending on whether the audience will want or require technical detail, whether they are looking for a summary of results, or whether they are about to examine your research in a Ph.D. exam.

— *The Story:* Every research project has at least one major "story" in it. Sometimes the story centres around a specific research finding. Sometimes it is based on a methodological problem or challenge. When you write your report, you should attempt to tell the "story" to your reader. Even in very formal journal articles where you will be required to be concise and detailed at the same time, a good "storyline" can help make an otherwise very dull report interesting to the reader.

The hardest part of telling the story in your research is finding the story in the first place. Usually when you come to writing up your research you have been steeped in the details for weeks or months. You've been worrying about sampling response, struggling with operationalising your measures, dealing with the details of design, and wrestling with the data analysis. You're a bit like the ostrich that has its head in the sand. To find the story in your research, you have to pull your head out of the sand and look at the big picture. You have to try to view your research from your audience's perspective. You may have to let go of some of the details that you obsessed so much about and leave them out of the write up or bury them in technical appendices or tables.

— *Formatting Considerations:* Are you writing a research report that you will submit for publication in a journal? If so, you should be aware that every journal requires articles that you follow specific formatting guidelines. Thinking of writing a book. Again, every publisher will require specific formatting.

ELEMENTS OR CRITERIA

This section describes the elements or criteria that you must typically address in a research paper. The assumption here is that you are addressing a causal hypothesis in your paper.

Introduction

— *Statement of the problem*: The general problem area is stated clearly and unambiguously. The importance and significance of the problem area is discussed.

— *Statement of causal relationship*: The cause-effect relationship to be studied is stated clearly and is sensibly related to the problem area.

— *Statement of constructs*: Each key construct in the research/evaluation project is explained (minimally, both the cause and effect). The explanations are readily understandable to an intelligent reader.

— *Literature citations and review*: The literature cited is from reputable and appropriate sources and you have a minimum of five references. The literature is condensed in an intelligent fashion with only the most relevant information included. Citations are in the correct format.

— *Statement of hypothesis*: The hypothesis is clearly stated and is specific about what is predicted. The relationship of the hypothesis to both the problem statement and literature review is readily understood from reading the text.

Methods

Sample Section

— *Sampling procedure specifications*: The procedure for selecting units for the study is described and is appropriate. The author state which sampling method is used and why. The population and sampling frame are described. In an evaluation, the programme participants are frequently self-selected and, if so, should be described as such.

— *Sample description*: The sample is described accurately and is appropriate. Problems in contacting and measuring the sample are anticipated.

— *External validity considerations*: Generalisability from the sample to the sampling frame and population is considered.

Measurement Section

— *Measures*: Each outcome measurement construct is described briefly (a minimum of two outcome constructs is required). For each construct, the measure or measures are described briefly and an appropriate citation and reference is included (unless you created the measure). You describe briefly the measure you constructed and provide the entire measure in an Appendix. The measures which are used are relevant to the hypotheses of the study and are included in those hypotheses. Wherever possible, multiple measures of the same construct are used.

— *Construction of measures*: For questionnaires, tests and interviews: questions are clearly worded, specific, appropriate for the population, and follow in a logical fashion. The standards for good questions are followed. For archival data: original data collection procedures are adequately described and indices are constructed correctly. For scales, you must describe briefly which scaling procedure you used and how you implemented it. For qualitative measures, the procedures for collecting the measures are described in detail.

— *Reliability and validity*: You must address both the reliability and validity of all of your measures. For reliability, you must specify what estimation procedure(s) you used. For validity, you must explain how you assessed construct validity. Wherever possible, you should minimally address both convergent and discriminant validity. The procedures which are used to examine reliability and validity are appropriate for the measures.

Design and Procedures Section:

— *Design*: The design is clearly presented in both notational and text form. The design is appropriate for the problem and addresses the hypothesis.

— *Internal validity*: Threats to internal validity and how they are addressed by the design are discussed. Any threats to internal validity which are not well controlled are also considered.

— *Description of procedures*: An overview of how the study will be conducted is included. The sequence of events is described and is appropriate to the design. Sufficient information is included so that the essential features of the study could be replicated by a reader.

Results

— Statement of Results: The results are stated concisely and are plausible for the research described.

— Tables: The table(s) is correctly formatted and accurately and concisely presents part of the analysis.

— Figures: The figure(s) is clearly designed and accurately describes a relevant aspect of the results.

Conclusions, Abstract and Reference Sections

— *Implications of the study*: Assuming the expected results are obtained, the implications of these results are discussed. The author mentions briefly any remaining problems which are anticipated in the study.

— *Abstract*: The Abstract is 125 words or less and presents a concise picture of the proposed research.

Major constructs and hypotheses are included. The Abstract is the first section of the paper.

— *References*: All citations are included in the correct format and are appropriate for the study described.

STYLISTIC ELEMENTS

Professional Writing

First person and sex-stereotyped forms are avoided. Material is presented in an unbiased and unemotional, but not necessarily uninteresting, fashion.

Parallel Construction

Tense is kept parallel within and between sentences (as appropriate).

Sentence Structure

Sentence structure and punctuation are correct. Incomplete and run-on sentences are avoided.

Spelling and Word Usage

Spelling and use of words are appropriate. Words are capitalised and abbreviated correctly.

General Style

The document is neatly produced and reads well. The format for the document has been correctly followed.

FORMATTING

The instructions provided here are for a research article or a research report. Please consult the specific guidelines that are required by the publisher for the type of document you are producing.

All sections of the paper should be typed, double-spaced on white 8 1/2 x 11 inch paper with 12 pitch typeface with all margins set to 1 inch. Every page must have a header in the upper right corner with the running header right-justified on the top line and the page number right-justified and double-spaced on the line below it. The paper must have all the sections in the order given below, following the specifications outlined for each section:

Title Page

On separate lines and centred, the title page has the title of the study, the author's name, and the institutional affiliation. At the bottom of the title page you should have the words (in caps): followed by a short identifying title (2-4 words) for the study. This running header should also appear on the top right of every page of the paper.

Abstract

The abstract is limited to one page, double-spaced. At the top of the page, centred, you should have the word 'Abstract'. The abstract itself should be written in paragraph form and should be a concise summary of the entire paper including: the problem; major hypotheses; sample and population; a brief description of the measures; the name of the design or a short description; the major results; and, the major conclusions. Obviously, to fit this all on one page you will have to be very concise.

Body

The first page of the body of the paper should have, centred, the complete title of the study.

Introduction

The first section in the body is the introduction. There is no heading that says 'Introduction,' you simply begin the paper in paragraph form following the title. Every introduction will have the following: a statement of the problem being addressed; a statement of the cause-effect relationship being studied; a description of the major constructs involved; a brief review of relevant literature; and a statement of hypotheses. The entire section should be in paragraph form with the possible exception of the hypotheses, which may be indented.

Methods

The next section of the paper has four subsections: Sample; Measures; Design; and, Procedure. The Methods section should begin immediately after the introduction and should have the centred title 'Methods'. Each of the four subsections should have an underlined left justified section heading.

Sampling

This section should describe the population of interest, the sampling frame, the method for selecting the sample, and the sample itself. A brief discussion of external validity is appropriate here, that is, you should state the degree to which you believe results will be generalisable from your sample to the population.

Measures

This section should include a brief description of your constructs and all measures that will be used to operationalise them. You may present short instruments in their entirety in this section. If you have more lengthy instruments you may present some "typical" questions to give the reader a sense of what you will be doing. You may include any instruments in full in appendices rather than in the body. Appendices should be labelled by letter and cited appropriately in the body of the text.

For pre-existing instruments you should cite any relevant information about reliability and validity if it is available. For all instruments, you should briefly state how you will determine reliability and validity, report the results and discuss. For reliability, you must describe the methods you used and report results. A brief discussion of how you have addressed construct validity is essential. In general, you should try to demonstrate both convergent and discriminant validity. You must discuss the evidence in support of the validity of your measures.

Design

You should state the name of the design that is used and tell whether it is a true or quasi-experiment, nonequivalent group design, and so on. You should also present the design structure in X and O notation (this should be indented and centred, not put into a sentence). You should also include a discussion of internal validity that describes the major likely threats in your study and how the design accounts for them, if at all.

Procedures

Generally, this section ties together the sampling, measurement, and research design. In this section you should briefly describe the overall plan of the research, the sequence of events from beginning to end, how participants will be notified, and how their confidentiality will be protected. An essential part of this subsection is a description of the programme or independent variable that you are studying.

Results

The heading for this section is centred with upper and lower case letters. You should indicate concisely what results you found in this research. Your results don't have to confirm your hypotheses. In fact, the common experience in social research is the finding of no effect.

Conclusions

Here you should describe the conclusions you reach (assuming you got the results described in the Results section above). You should relate these conclusions back to the level of the construct and the general problem area which you described in the Introduction section. You should also discuss the overall strength of the research proposed and should present some suggestions for possible future research which would be sensible based on the results of this work.

References

There are really two parts to a reference citation. First, there is the way you cite the item in the text when you are discussing it. Second, there is the way you list the complete reference in the reference section in the back of the report.

Reference Citations in the Text of Your Paper: Cited references appear in the text of your paper and are a way of giving credit to the source of the information or quote you have used in your paper.

Bibliography

Berg, B.L., *Qualitative Research Methods for the Social Sciences*, Allyn and Bacon, 1989.

Borg, W.R., and Gall, M.D., *Educational Research: An Introduction*, (Fifth edition) Longman, 1989.

Breakwell, G.M., Hammond, S., and Fife-Schaw, C. (Eds.), *Research Methods in Psychology*, Sage, 1995.

Bruning, J.L., and Kintz, B.L., *Computational Handbook of Statistics*, (Third edition) Scott, Foresman, 1987.

Bulmer, M., *Sociological Research Methods*, (Second edition) Macmillan, 1984.

Campbell, D.T., and Stanley, J.C., "Experimental and quasi-experimental designs for research," In: N.L. Gage (Ed.) *Handbook of Research on Teaching*, Rand McNally, 1963.

Cohen, L., and Manion, I., *Research Methods in Education*, Routledge, 1989.

Denzin, N.K., and Lincoln, Y.S. (Eds.), *Handbook of Qualitative Research*, Sage, 1994.

Dominowski, R.L., *Research Methods*, Prentice-Hall, 1980.

Ely, M., Anzul, M., Friedman, T., Garner, D., and Steinmetz, A.M., *Doing Qualitative Research: Circles within Circles*, Falmer Press, 1990.

Hakim, C., *Research Design: Strategies and Choices in the Design of Social Research*, Allen and Unwin, 1987.

Isaac, S., and Michael, W.B., *Handbook in Research and Evaluation for Education and the Behavioural Sciences*, EdITS Publishers, 1989.

Kahneman, D., Slovic, P., and Tversky, A., *Judgment under Uncertainty: Heuristics and Biases*, Cambridge University Press, 1982.

Kraemer, K.L. (Ed.), *The Information Systems Research Challenge: Survey Research Methods*, Volume 3, Harvard Business School, 1989.

Maykut, P., and Morehouse, R., *Beginning Qualitative Research: A Philosophical and Practical Guide*, Falmer Press, 1994.

Moser, C.A., and Kalton, G., *Survey Methods of Social Investigation*, Gower, 1979.

Oppenheim, A.N., *Questionnaire Design, Interviewing and Attitutde Measurement*, Pinter, 1993.

Riley, J., *Getting the Most from Your Data: A Handbook of Practical Ideas on How to Analyse Qualitative Data*, Bristol: Technical and Educational Services Ltd., 1990.

Robson, C., *Real World Research: A Resource for Social Scientists and Practitioner-Researchers*, Blackwell, 1993.

Silverman, D., *Interpreting Qualitative Data*, Sage, 1993.

Strauss, A., *Qualitative Analysis for Social Scientists*, Cambridge University Press, 1987.

Sinha Suresh C. and Anil K. Dhiman, *Research Methodology*, New Delhi, Ess Ess, 2002.

Singh, Yogesh Kumar, Ruchika Nath, *Research Methodology*, Year Of Publication : 2005.

Taylor Bill, Gautam Sinha, Taposh Ghoshal, *Research Methodology: A Guide for Researchers in Management and Social Sciences*, Prentice-Hall of India Private Limited, New Delhi 2006.

Tesch, R., *Qualitative Research: Analysis Types & Software Tools*, Falmer Press, 1990.

Index

□□□

34.	Science Teaching in Schools	175/-
35.	Indian National Congress (New)	450/-
36.	Indian Polity (Revised Edition)	295/-
37.	New Comparative Government (Revised Edition)	295/-
	Advanced Study in the History of Modern India	
38.	(Volume-1: 1707-1813)	225/-
39.	(Volume-2: 1813-1920)	325/-
40.	(Volume-3: 1920-1947)	175/-
41.	Handbook of Nutrition & Dietetics	250/-
42.	Development of Education in India	195/-
43.	A Text Book of Environmental Studies	195/-
44.	Teaching of History	175/-
45.	Administrative Thinkers	195/-
46.	Research Methodology	175/-
47.	Curriculum Development	195/-
48.	Teaching of Science	175/-
49.	Teaching of Mathematics	175/-
50.	Principles of Educational &Vocational Guidance	195/-
51.	Child Psychology	175/-
52.	Abnormal Psychology	175/-
53.	Indian Education in Emerging Society	195/-
54.	Human Resource Management	175/-
55.	Higher Education and Global Challenges	175/-
56.	Teaching of Geography	175/-
57.	Teaching of Social Studies	175/-
58.	Teaching of English	175/-
59.	Principles of Office Management (Revised Edition)	250/-
60.	Education for All The Indian Saga	175/-
61.	Value Education in Global Perspective	195/-
62.	Teacher Training	175/-
63.	Public Administration	175/-
64.	Public Relations & Integrated Communications	195/-
65.	Educational Psychology	175/-
66.	Introduction to Educational Technology	175/-
67.	Textbook of Food and Nutrition	175/-

Lotus PRESS

Unit No. 220, 2nd Floor, 4735/22,
Prakash Deep Building,Ansari Road, Darya Ganj,
New Delhi- 110002, Ph.: 32903912, 23280047, 09811594448
• E-mail : lotus_press@sify.com, www.lotuspress.co.in